# Managing Local
# Government Archives

# Managing Local Government Archives

John H. Slate
Kaye Lanning Minchew

ROWMAN & LITTLEFIELD
Lanham • Boulder • New York • London

Published by Rowman & Littlefield
A wholly owned subsidiary of The Rowman & Littlefield Publishing Group, Inc.
4501 Forbes Boulevard, Suite 200, Lanham, Maryland 20706
www.rowman.com

Unit A, Whitacre Mews, 26-34 Stannary Street, London SE11 4AB

British Library Cataloguing in Publication Information Available

**Library of Congress Cataloging-in-Publication Data**

Names: Slate, John H., author. | Minchew, Kaye Lanning, author.
Title: Managing local government archives / John H. Slate [and] Kaye Lanning Minchew.
Description: Lanham, Maryland : Rowman & Littlefield, 2016. | Includes bibliographical references and index.
Identifiers: LCCN 2016002708 (print) | LCCN 2016008726 (ebook) | ISBN 9781442263949 (cloth : alk. paper) | ISBN 9781442263956 (pbk. : alk. paper) | ISBN 9781442263963 (electronic)
Subjects: LCSH: Local government—United States—Records and correspondence—Management. | Municipal government—United States—Records and correspondence—Management. | Public records—United States—Management. | Archival resources—United States—Management.
Classification: LCC JS344.P77 S58 2016 (print) | LCC JS344.P77 (ebook) | DDC 025.1/975—dc23
LC record available at http://lccn.loc.gov/2016002708

$\infty$™ The paper used in this publication meets the minimum requirements of American National Standard for Information Sciences—Permanence of Paper for Printed Library Materials, ANSI/NISO Z39.48-1992.

Printed in the United States of America

This book is dedicated to our families and to David B. Gracy II, a wonderful mentor and friend; and to our fellow local government archivists who share, commiserate, and work to make the permanent records of local government archives transparent and accessible.

# Contents

# Foreword

Since the publication of my book *Local Government Records* thirty-five years ago, record-keeping at all levels of government has undergone evolutionary changes, especially with the advent of digitization. The challenge, however, remains the same: to preserve records of continuing value and to orderly and legally dispose of those that have served their purpose. In *Managing Local Government Archives*, John Slate and Kaye Minchew, both certified archivists, provide guidance to local officials often too busy to give much thought to "old records" as they are moved out of sight.

It is at the local level that our rights and privileges as citizens are documented: birth, marriage, death, property ownership, right to vote. It is at the local level, too, that vital records may be crowded out by the absence of an orderly disposal of those without continuing value. This book will be of assistance to county, municipal, and other local officials generally, but it will serve its greatest purpose as a reminder that records are public property and deserve to be treated accordingly. An "archival saint," Waldo Gifford Leland, put it this way: "The chief monument of the history of a nation is its archives, the preservation of which is recognized by all civilized countries as a natural and proper function of government." The same applies to the permanently valuable records of state and local governments

Texas and Georgia, the domiciles of the authors, are governed by 254 counties and 159 counties respectively and contain thousands of localities in various categories and sizes, each with its unique history, geography, and traditions. Other states have fewer record-producing units, but their officials, like those in Texas and Georgia, will find *Managing Local Government Archives* helpful in recognizing their role in assuring that the American experience is documented by the preservation of our documentary heritage.

Unlike *Local Government Records*, which dealt heavily with the legal aspects of public records, *Managing Local Government Archives* is concerned primarily with records that mature into "archives"—that is, those with values beyond their immediate administrative value. As such, the book will provide a useful tool for officers and custodians genuinely interested in the records that inexorably accumulate in their office.

H. G. Jones
Pittsboro, North Carolina

# Preface

*Managing Local Government Archives* is the result of some ten years of thought and discussion. As professional archivists working with local government archives and records, we wondered for some time why there were no full-length books on this subject, save for H. G. Jones's 1980 book *Local Government Records: An Introduction to Their Management, Preservation, and Use*. It's a great book and contains information that is still relevant, but, of course, much has changed since 1980. Inspired by the dearth of published literature and the tenacity of our colleagues in the field, we felt this area of archives deserved a book-length treatment that went beyond tip sheets and case studies.

Some things, however, never seem to change. With only a few exceptions, most local government archives programs are still staffed by only a few people and most often by "lone arrangers." Many times, people suddenly have responsibility for caring for local government archives with very little archival education or training. The purpose of this book is to expand and update some of the themes in H. G. Jones's work, and to introduce some facets of archival work that he did not touch upon. More than anything else, we wanted to produce a book that contains practical information. There is a place for books and articles on theory, but we want people working with local government records to learn from real-life experiences. We know that staffing and budgets are usually limited and choices have to be made, especially when establishing a local archives program.

Both of us have worked in archives environments for over thirty years each, most of it within local governments. We know how exciting, challenging, and sometimes frustrating local government archives can be. We have gained much experience from day-to-day work, and even more from visiting archives around the country and the world and talking with archivists about their work. From the archives of ancient cities like Istanbul and Budapest to the archives of younger governments in the United States such as Seattle and much newer cities and counties, we have observed a wide variety of archival settings and many different issues that come up within local governments.

We hope that more and more governments realize they have both a legal obligation to take care of permanent records as well as a moral obligation to citizens and researchers to make their archival holdings open and transparent. To provide assistance to archivists and governments across the country and the world, we present our thoughts grounded in hard-earned experience.

# Acknowledgments

We have been discussing the need for a new volume about local government archives for several years. In too many communities across the United States, local government archives continue to be lost due to neglect and deplorable conditions.

We would like to express our gratitude to the many people who saw us through this book: to all those who provided support, talked things over, read, wrote, offered comments, and allowed us to quote their remarks. We especially thank our colleagues in the Government Records Section and the Local Government Records Round Table of the Society of American Archivists and the National Association of Government Archivists and Records Administrators for their support and advice.

We would like to thank the following people for their advice and counsel: Jelain Chubb, state archivist, and Mark Myers, Texas State Library and Archives Commission; Dr. David B. Gracy II; Geof Huth, New York State Unified Court System; H. G. Jones; Kate Theimer; Paul R. Scott, and Sarah Canby Jackson, Harris County (TX) Archives and Records Management; Lois Dillard, Dallas Municipal Archives and Records Center; Thomas F. R. Clareson, Lyrasis; and Scott Cline, Seattle Municipal Archives.

For images, we thank the following agencies and individuals: the Louisiana Division/City Archives, New Orleans Public Library; John J. McColgan and the City of Boston Archives; Salt Lake County Health Department; the Dallas Municipal Archives, Dallas, Texas; Walter Hinick, the *Montana Standard*; Diana Banning and the City of Portland (OR) Archives and Records Center; the *Dallas Morning News*; Terry Baxter and the Multnomah County (OR) Archives; Harris County (TX) Archives; Tattnall County Archives Committee; Baldwin County (AL) Archives; Anne S. Floyd, Central Savannah River Area

Regional Commission; Richard B. Trask and the Danvers Archival Center, Danvers, Massachusetts; and Clayton, County (GA) Archives and Records.

We would like to thank Charles Harmon for his role as editor.

Above all we thank our families, who supported and encouraged us in spite of all the time it took us away from them.

This list of acknowledgments can only capture a small fraction of the people who supported our work. We send our deep thanks to all. Your contributions to this book were vital, but the inevitable mistakes in it are very much our own.

John H. Slate and Kaye Lanning Minchew

# Introduction

There are now just over eighty-nine thousand local governments in the United States. Some of these governments have active archives programs. Other permanently valuable local government records are under the care of historical societies and similar groups. But there are many more bodies of records languishing in unsuitable storage, under poor conditions for long-term preservation. Most of these places are also staffed by nonprofessionals, who cannot be faulted for lack of support or lack of experience. While there is a long and proud history of local archives programs, it is a sobering fact that the vast majority of local government archives do not have the support of their governments, in spite of their incalculable value and worth. Governments, individual employees, and responsible citizens must do whatever is within their means to protect and preserve these valuable assets of American history.

What is a "local government" archives? What is the definition of a local government? Why are they important? How should a local government archives be managed? This book seeks to help the reader understand what comprises local government archives and how they operate, and to offer suggestions for how to manage them.

We would like to begin with two scenarios. In the first, a county's governing body has discovered that the county government will reach its two hundredth anniversary soon. County leaders have declared that there must be a great roundup of historical items that mark the many milestones in its history. In the absence of an archives program, the task is delegated to a committee of well-meaning county employees who must work with each of the fifty departments of the county to find interesting and historic things to use in publication and display. Some departments have squirreled away their history and are glad to share. Others have no sense of history and have destroyed many years of documentation.

In the second scenario, a city government has been plunged into a crisis involving city-owned land in a densely populated, older section of the city. The real estate was donated many years earlier by a citizen and is now used as a municipal golf course. But now her descendants have decided the terms of the donation were not followed and the land should be returned to the family. The deeds have been located, but is there more information the city needs to protect its assets? The municipal archives retrieved correspondence documenting the early transactions during the acquisition. In one folder, the donor's telegram approving of the land use settles once and for all the question of intention, thereby saving countless citizen tax dollars in legal fees, as well as protecting a cherished public park.

The first scenario represents the missed opportunities and readiness that would have made the county government shine had it already established a functioning archival program. Hundreds of hours could have been saved, and gaps in the historical record might not exist if the archives had been actively locating and identifying records of permanent and historical value.

The second scenario represents the importance of archives in the protection of public assets—in this case, public park lands. Without proof of intent, the land would have reverted back to the donor's heirs, and a historic park and golf course might have become a lucrative private real estate investment and a tremendous loss to the city.

This book was written under the premise that the vast majority of the people in charge of the majority of our nation's local government archives have very little formal training in caring for records—and may never have such training. We hope to promote clear thinking about preservation, management, and use. Regardless of the size of your archival holding, there are things you should be doing and a variety of ways for your archives to serve staff within the government and the general public. Our goal is to anticipate your questions and suggest good practices for dealing with a wide variety of archival issues, including electronic records, outreach and exhibits, and assuring the long-term preservation of your documents with proper facilities and storage supplies. While there isn't enough room in one book to go into great detail, it is a starting point. The book's chapters include references to printed and online resources, plus appendixes with an example of enabling legislation to establish local government archives programs as well as samples of forms commonly found in local government archives.

It is almost self-evident that every state and territory in the United States has valuable local history. For instance, Texas has 254 counties and Georgia has 159. Each one of those counties has a courthouse. And within each of those courthouses are records of historic and enduring value. Some of those counties contain the history of settlements that date back four hundred years. Located in each of those counties are one to many municipalities. There are also other kinds of local government entities, such as school districts, water districts, transportation authorities, and industrial development authorities. Out of those thousands of governing bodies, only a few have funded and staffed archives programs. In an ideal society, every government would have a formal archives and would care for their permanently valuable records, making their contents available for public and internal use.

Why do we need archives? To paraphrase Bruce Dearstyne's points in *The Management of Local Government Records: A Guide for Local Officials,*

- Archives are important to the study of history.
- Archives protect the rights of individuals and provide transparency.
- Archives protect the assets of local governments.
- Archives save governmental departments time and money in everyday operations.[1]

The records originally created by a government were made to serve as evidence of transactions. By preserving public records created by governmental bodies as archives, local governments preserve institutional memory and evidence of transactions, as well as the context related to the activity. Information about the past informs our decision making now and in the future.

Public records are like no other kind of record because they *belong* to the public. They are created with public funds by employees paid with public funds, and thus are fully accountable to citizens. As former North Carolina state archivist H. G. Jones stated, "Public records are public property, owned by the people in the same sense that citizens own their courthouse or town hall, sidewalks, and streets, funds in the treasury. They are held in trust for the citizens by custodians."[2]

The Council of State Archivists declared that local government records are the records "closest to home" in their 2007–2011 study. They are the records that most directly and most often touch our lives as citizens and residents of municipalities and states across the country. Local governments are where the original copy of our marriage certificates are filed, just as are divorce decrees. The plans and building inspection records from our homes and businesses are usually part of a permanent file kept by our local government. Our daily lives are reflected in local government records—civil and criminal court records; deeds; marriage, estate, and tax materials; and many more types of permanent records—which tell us about ourselves and about others.

Local government archives protect the rights of citizens and are a part of a local identity. A properly operated local government archives promotes efficient and accountable government. Public records and archives also create transparency, which is a cornerstone of democratic values.

Over time, local government records document a government from its creation to modern day while serving as the official corporate memory of the government and its people. Equally important, the history of the government and its policies and the enforcement of these policies are documented by archives and mirror-shifting societal values. Archives form a wealth of information used regularly by local residents, historians, genealogists, government officials, attorneys, surveyors, legal researchers, and others.

In too many cases, archival records in local governments across the nation have accumulated over the decades and centuries with little thought to their preservation or long-term care. Local records, despite their significance, are typically among the most neglected records in the nation.

Historians and archivists have decried the lack of adequate care for historical records but staff in local governments continue to face many challenges in their preservation. Lack of staff and funding and, perhaps worse, lack of administrative support make caring for archives difficult and sometimes unmanageable. Indifference and neglect are reflected in misfiling, damage, and even outright destruction. Without proper storage and environment, it is little wonder that the crisis in local government archives has remained an untamed tiger.

One more example helps illustrate the frustration that is too often encountered in local governments. In the shadow of our nation's federal government sits the District of Columbia Archives. Its historic and permanently valuable records include birth and death records, wills, land records, and marriage records. With little support, the archives suffered years of neglect and poor storage conditions, despite holding the original wills of Alexander Graham Bell, Francis Scott Key, James Madison, Dolley Madison, Woodrow Wilson, Oliver Wendell Holmes, and Frederick Douglass, as well as the birth certificates for such famous District figures as Duke Ellington.

Floods and fire compounded the archives' problems. After several years of public pressure, a public support group was created, made up of archivists, historians, D.C. government employees, and interested citizens, who encouraged the D.C. government to increase funding for the archives. The increased funding has been dedicated to a new facility, which will spotlight the importance of proper storage environment, the need to celebrate and display its treasures, and better prepare for the future with electronic records.[3]

Although archival records comprise only a small percentage of the total volume of records created by a local government, they are usually among the most important files created for citizens, researchers and government staff members. Archival records may consist of handwritten leather-bound volumes of minutes dating from the early days of the government or may be the minutes of last week's council meeting in electronic form.

The value of local government archives in society and in the writing of history cannot be overestimated. In *Documenting Localities*, author Richard Cox notes that "the most interesting and provocative reason for the interest in local history has probably been the significance of the locality to the individual's own self-identity, not dissimilar to the reasons why genealogy and family history have grown in popularity in the same last quarter of a century."[4] He further added that "the significance of the locality for understanding our past and present demands better and more systematic work than it seems we have provided."[5]

This book is a whole-hearted attempt to effect change in the preservation and accessibility of local government archives.

## NOTES

1. Bruce W. Dearstyne, *The Management of Local Government Records* (Nashville, TN: American Association for State and Local History, 1988), 104–5.

2. H. G. Jones, *Local Government Records: An Introduction to Their Management, Preservation, and Use* (Nashville, TN: American Association of State and Local History, 1980), 23.

3. Anthony L. Harvey, "Long-Neglected Attention to Decaying Archives Building and Holdings Finally Reversed as New Mayor and City Council Commit to Funding," *The InTowner* (Washington, DC), June 13, 2015.

4. Richard J. Cox, *Documenting Localities* (Chicago: Society of American Archivists and Scarecrow Press, 1996), 15.

5. Cox, *Documenting Localities*, 27.

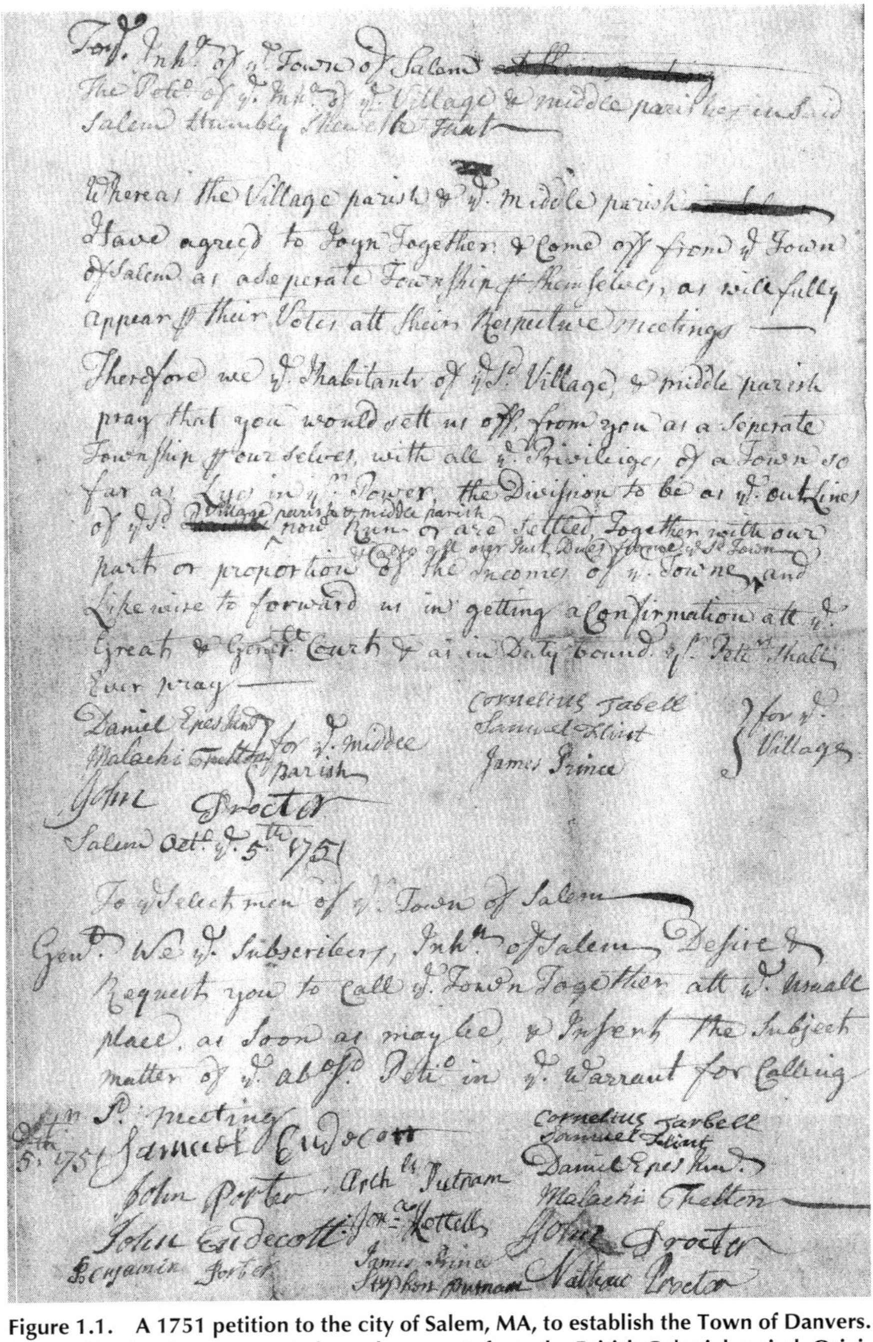

**Figure 1.1.** A 1751 petition to the city of Salem, MA, to establish the Town of Danvers. Many older local governments have documents from the British Colonial period. Originally called Salem Village, Danvers is best known as the site of the Salem Witch Trials of 1692. Image courtesy Danvers Archival Center, Danvers, Massachusetts.

# A Short History of Local Government and Local Government Archives in the United States

The history of local government archives in the United States is as diverse as the history of colonization, settlement, and westward expansion on the North American continent itself. On the Atlantic coast there are local governments with records dating back four hundred years, while in the far western states there are governments that are barely one hundred years old. The key to understanding the nature of the archives of a local government is to understand where that government's record-keeping traditions originated. While today there is a fairly high level of uniformity in the organization of local governments, it wasn't always the case in the beginning. Many laws and record-keeping customs in the former Thirteen Colonies that have roots in English governmental models are markedly different from those found in other parts of the present United States whose local governments were originally established under Spanish, Mexican, German, or French rule.

It is also a matter of interpretation as to what constitutes a *local* government. Because of the lack of autonomy in royal hierarchies, neither Spanish nor British colonial governments had anything resembling what is today known as a municipal corporation. The Spanish colonial concept of municipality included a settlement as well as surrounding territory that could be hundreds or thousands of square miles. In some places such as Texas, Spanish colonial municipalities were in fact the origin of some present-day counties.[1] With few exceptions, Britain does not have incorporated municipalities, but instead relies upon a structure of metropolitan districts, boroughs, counties, and civil parishes as the recognized lower units of local government. Reform legislation in England in 1835, 1882, 1883, 1972, and 1986 regularized or changed the legal status of local governments, but to this day concepts of local government in England do not fully correspond to the American municipal or county government.[2]

## LOCAL GOVERNMENTS IN THE BRITISH COLONIES

A brief overview of the organization of local governments in the British North American colonies provides a microcosmic example of how to approach the historical organization of local governments and, by extension, their documents of enduring value. After the first permanent settlement at Jamestown in 1607, the British monarchy permitted individuals and groups exclusive rights to establish colonies on the Atlantic coast. These are still called the Thirteen Colonies and fall into two basic kinds of governments—corporation and provincial. Massachusetts, Rhode Island, and Connecticut are examples of corporation colonies; examples of provincial colonies, which include proprietary and royal charters, are Maryland, Pennsylvania, Delaware, Virginia, the Carolinas, New Hampshire, Vermont, New Jersey, and Georgia.[3]

At the time of British colonization, England's local government tradition was derived from the Saxons, most famously credited as the uniters of the various kingdoms making up the British Isles. *Counties*, which are the largest administrative unit of forty-eight states in the United States, derive from a somewhat similar geopolitical division found in Great Britain and Ireland and were originally a territory under the administration of a count or earl (hence the etymology of "county"). In both Great Britain and the United States, counties exercise administrative, judicial, and political functions. The only states of the United States that do not have counties are Louisiana and Alaska. Louisiana contains parishes, which are the equivalent of counties but have retained much of their heritage and some of their structure from Roman Catholic France and Spain. Alaska is organized into boroughs and census areas.

The *borough* is a self-governing administrative unit of government whose concept has multiple definitions depending upon time and place. Believed to have originated in the Germanic *burg* (fort), the British idea of borough dates to the Middle Ages and was a settlement or town granted semiautonomous status from the Crown. Neither county nor municipality, boroughs in the United States have functions of both types of local government. A borough can be defined as a municipal corporation that is created when a county is merged with populated areas within it.[4] Seven states (Alaska, Connecticut, Minnesota, New Jersey, New York, Pennsylvania, and Virginia) contain borough governments, though they vary greatly in resemblance to municipalities or counties. The best-known examples of boroughs in the United States are the five divisions of New York City.

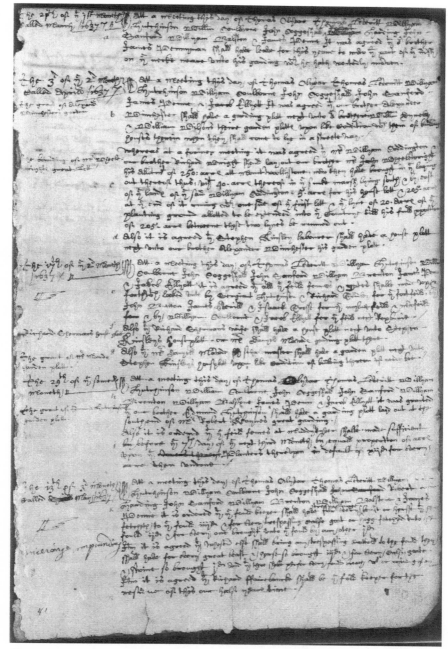

Figure 1.2. A 1637 page from the earliest records of the City of Boston, Massachusetts, relates to assigning lots for constructing houses. Early archival records of local governments explain how towns and cities were organized. Image courtesy City of Boston Archives.

The county and borough units of government were in use in Great Britain and Ireland by approximately 1300, and within them grew townships, towns and shires, which governed themselves by means of locally elected councils.

*Parishes* were ecclesiastical units of government created by the Church of England, were governed by local parish councils or vestries, and were responsible for local road upkeep and a simple welfare system for the indigent based on the national "poor laws" of 1601 and their reformation in 1834.[5] Examples of the kinds of bodies and records found in British colonial local government archives include Clerk of the Peace, County Courts, Courts of Quarter Sessions, Court of Common Pleas, probate records, birth and death registers, and other lists and registers of great variety (e.g., land tax assessments, registry of deeds, freeholders lists).

Parishes in Louisiana little resemble the parish system of Great Britain. After the United States designated Louisiana as the Territory of Orleans in 1804, it was divided into a county system, which did not work well. In 1807 the territory reorganized its civil government roughly according to Roman Catholic parishes in the region. The governing body of the parish is called the Police Jury, which is both the legislative and executive local government. Though not every parish is governed by a Police Jury, forty-one of the sixty-four parishes use this system. Instead of Police Juries, some parishes are governed by parish councils or parish commissions.[6]

The Police Jury is analogous to the commission or council that govern a county. Its elected officials are called Jurors, and include a president. Parish judges and justices of the peace are other appointed officials. The office of sheriff was added in 1810. When Louisiana was admitted to the Union in 1812, the state kept the parish system. Parishes are further subdivided into wards. The Louisiana Constitution of 1975 further codified and formalized the parish system as it exists today.[7]

In the Spanish and Mexican-ruled parts of North America, rudimentary semiautonomous municipal governments existed under the Franciscan Order and under military rule, and derived concepts of government from Spanish traditions. *Pueblos* were civil settlements associated with missions and presidios on the frontier. Pueblos often grew to become *villas* (towns) or *ciudades* (cities). These governments consisted of an *ayuntamiento* or *cabildo* (council) whose officers included an *alcalde* (judge), an appointive body of aldermen or councilors known as *regidores*, a *síndico procurador* (attorney) who often also acted as *mayordomo de propios* (administrator of public lands), an *alguacil* (sheriff), and an *escribano* (secretary and keeper of records).[8] This form of government lacked the office of mayor, though the role of chief executive was essentially included in the duties of the *alcalde ordinario*.[9] Kinds of records found in Spanish colonial local government archives include ordinances and laws, vital statistics, allotments of land, tax renditions, wills, settlements of estates, and civil and criminal case files. Many of these documents are found assembled in the most common file unit of Spanish archives, the *legajo*, a bundle of loose papers tied together with string and kept together by subject matter. A page from a legajo is called a *folio*.[10]

What is uniquely American, however, is the concept of a municipal corporation. Cities in England were authorized to operate by means of a royal charter. Municipal corporations are organized under the laws of the state. Under state law, municipalities are granted the power to provide infrastructure services, legislate public health and safety, and tax and collect fees for certain kinds of licensing and services as long as they do not conflict with state or federal law. State laws also use population density to determine legal status, with separate laws and powers for a city, town, borough, and village.

Historically, many of the functions of municipalities today were once performed by different units of government, but now are encompassed under one umbrella. The California League of Women Voters, for example, defines a city government as "responsible for providing services which directly affect the lives of their residents. Through fire and police protection, cities safeguard lives and property. They also construct and maintain streets, provide facilities for sewage, storm drainage, and waste disposal, and look after health, recreational and social needs. Most cities provide water; some provide public transportation systems; a few manage municipal utilities such as electricity or natural gas. City planning and zoning determine land use compatible with community economic, environmental, and cultural goals."[11] In a number of places, there are city-county partnerships to fund and administer such things as hospitals, transportation and water districts, and other services.

Besides understanding older governmental structures, it is also worthwhile to become familiar with the kinds of record-keeping formats used at different times and by different nationalities. Studying the origins of forms and their use sheds much light on how governments conducted day to day business two hundred years ago and more.

## LOCAL GOVERNMENTS WITH MULTINATIONAL CUSTOMS

Many local governments in the United States are the product of multinational customs and practices. Louisiana and Texas are particularly unusual examples of diversity in local government history because, since settlement by Europeans, parts of these two states have been under the rule of six different entities at one time or another. The early records of the City of San Antonio, Texas, for instance, are Spanish in origin but later came under the rule of the

Mexican government. After independence from Mexico, San Antonio was a major city in the independent Republic of Texas, the twenty-eighth state to enter the Union, and briefly a state in the Confederate States of America. In these last three instances, local governments were largely modeled on Anglo-American customs and practices. When California became a state in 1850, at least one county—San Luis Obispo—actually retained some of the offices of Spanish and Mexican origin for a time.[12]

Louisiana's local governments have an equally exotic pedigree. Under French rule (1699–1769) and Spanish rule (1769–1803), a royal notary recorded civil court documents, sometimes called notarial or succession records, for the Louisiana colony. Many of the military outposts—such as Opelousas, Attakapas, Natchitoches, or Natchez—had commandants who served as de facto notaries and sent copies of documents to New Orleans whenever necessary.

Following the Louisiana Purchase in 1803, the Americans imposed Anglo-American government record-keeping practices. With the exception of notarial and judicial records, the French and Spanish sent their administrative records back to Europe. Over time the parish clerks of court became the caretakers of the abandoned notarial and judicial archives. New Orleans, being a larger city, had five: a Recorder of Mortgages, Registrar of Conveyances, Custodian of Notarial Archives, a Clerk of the Civil Court, and a Clerk of the Criminal Court.[13]

Other states with multinational governmental heritage include New York (Dutch and English); California (Spanish and Anglo-American); and New Mexico (Spanish, Mexican, and Anglo-American). Local self-governance in North America also includes American Indians, who have self-governing nations surpassing the geopolitical boundaries of the United States. The local governments of American Indian tribes did not begin keeping written records until the late eighteenth century and retained governance traditions specific to the tribe. Once languages acquired Westernized alphabets or tribes began transacting business in Spanish or English, their local governments accumulated paper records with permanent value. The Navajo Nation today, for example, has 110 chapters, which are the smallest administrative units of the nation's legislative branch and the closest analogue to a local government.

In a few cases, some early local governments evolved out of businesses. The Dutch colony of New Amsterdam, for example, was governed by the Dutch West India Company. Because it was a corporation and not a nation, the company's administrators under the Dutch Republic did not formalize local government until some thirty years after its founding. Only in 1646 did it grant municipal privileges to the "Village of Breuckelen" across the river from its primary trading post, New Amsterdam. According to the New York

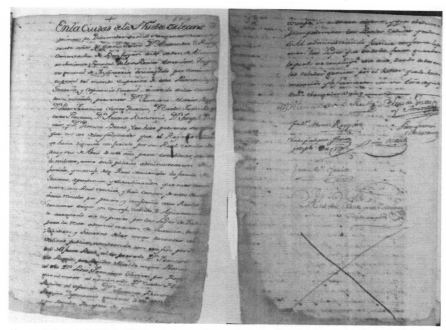

Figure 1.3. A 1769 local government document creating a Cabildo, or municipal government, for Spanish New Orleans. Recordkeeping traditions from Spain, France and England are represented in many local government archives. Image courtesy Louisiana Division/City Archives, New Orleans Public Library.

Department of State's *Local Government Handbook,* in 1653 the "Merchants and Elders of the Community of New Amsterdam" were permitted to establish what was called "a city government." This is the origin of the municipality later known as New York City.[14] Once surrendered to the British in 1664, the former local governments of New Netherland adopted English models of government.

## LOCAL GOVERNMENT ARCHIVES IN NONGOVERNMENTAL ENTITIES

Although a local government is the most logical place to find local government archives, that is not always the case. Some local government archival materials have resided outside their creating agencies for many years. Historical societies and organizations, libraries, and museums have collected government records as valued documentation of local government history, following in the historical manuscripts tradition begun in the late eighteenth century. Probably the earliest nongovernmental entity to collect and maintain local government records is the Massachusetts Historical Society, founded in 1791. The State Historical Society of Wisconsin, founded in 1846, is itself a state-supported agency that began collecting and making available local government records from its inception.

## HISTORICAL EVENTS AND FIGURES IN THE DEVELOPMENT OF LOCAL GOVERNMENT ARCHIVES

Most local government archives and records practices derive from the *public records tradition*, described by Richard C. Berner as distinct from the historical manuscripts tradition. Where historical manuscripts practices are more deeply rooted in librarianship, the public records tradition traces its professional origins to European and American governmental practices. The 1898 seminal work *Manual for the Arrangement and Description of Archives*, authored by Dutch archivists, is frequently cited as a core text in the development of archival theory, particularly in regard to government records. A year later, the American Historical Association initiated the Public Archives Commission to help define the inherent differences between private papers and public archives. The commission surveyed state archives between 1900 and 1917, many of which held archival records of local governments.[15]

While the day-to-day record-keeping habits of local governments changed little over the nineteenth and early twentieth centuries, the *organization* of local government archives for the purposes of historical research changed dramatically. The efforts of Waldo Gifford Leland and the American Historical Association greatly influenced archival practices, especially in the areas of provenance, arrangement, and description. Later refinements by the National Archives, the Library of Congress, and a number of individuals helped create the standards and customs of model local government archives and records programs.[16]

Federal policies, practices, and standards introduced from the 1930s through the 1970s significantly influenced the management of local government archives and records programs. A number of historic events on the federal level—some directly connected to local government, some less direct—have shaped the structure and business practices of local government archives. Awareness of the values of local government records accelerated in the 1930s when the National Archives (now the National Archives and Records Administration, or NARA) was created by Congress in 1934 to centralize federal record keeping. While the focus of its programs is primarily on federal records, the National Archives and other federal agencies like the Library of Congress developed methods of preservation and access for their own use that were incrementally adopted by state archives and historical societies.

In turn, state archives created local records programs to help municipal and county governments establish and apply records management and archives practices. Some states preceded the National Archives and provided formal local government assistance as far back as 1901 (Connecticut) and 1912 (New York), a few in the 1930s (Indiana, Maryland), but most started anywhere from the late 1940s to the early 1970s. Margaret Cross Norton, Illinois state archivist, developed some of the first descriptions of records series during the late 1930s, providing a model for the organization of local archival materials, at the same time as for state records.[17]

The National Archives and several of its staff have had a lasting influence on local government archives practices. Emmett J. Leahy (1910–1964) was influential in his work with the National Archives in the 1930s and the Office of the Secretary of the Navy in the 1940s, where he promoted the reduction of records in government through such practices as disposal authorization, transfer to archival custody, sampling and microfilming, data integrity review, and the general segregation of records having no permanent value. In helping define the records management profession, Leahy helped make clearer distinctions between government records of enduring value and those of limited, non-permanent value. Leahy's innovations, such as the concept of commercial storage vendors, live on in businesses like Iron Mountain, Inc., formerly known as Pierce-Leahy.[18]

Another figure of note in the development of management of local government archives and records practices is Philip C. Brooks. Brooks (1906–1977) published *Public Records Management* in 1949 through the Chicago-based Public Administration Service. A National Archives employee and the first director of the Harry S. Truman Presidential Library, Brooks taught archival science at American University in Washington, D.C., provided consulting services to local governments, and served as president of the Society of American Archivists. As a consultant, his influence was felt in such places as Texas, where his 1946–1950 study of the Texas State Library records program helped form the foundation for a broad records management policy for the government of Texas. Included in the report was a recommendation to include a local government archives program.[19]

Archivists are more familiar with the work of T. R. Schellenberg. Schellenberg also had a "big picture" approach like Leahy and Brooks and embraced both archives and records management, but occupied most of his time and scholarship with matters of permanent government records. It is Schellenberg (1903–1970), pioneering archivist and theorist, who helped develop many archival practices, primarily in the area of appraisal. His influential books *Modern Archives* (1956) and the *Management of Archives* (1965) became required reading in archives training coursework. While most of his work was with federal records, Schellenberg also recognized the importance of local government archives, going so far as to develop a training program in the early 1960s for the Texas State Library and Archives through the University of Texas Graduate School of Library and Information Science.[20] It is Schellenberg to whom local government archivists can point as a proponent of limited arrangement and description, an idea revisited and renewed decades later in the "more product, less processing" writings of Mark Greene and Dennis Meissner.

Beyond individuals, a number of schools and training programs have impacted local government archives and records programs, such as the Modern Archives Institute. The institute was a cooperative effort with the Library of Congress, founded by National Archives staff member Ernst Posner in 1945. It was originally sponsored by not only the National Archives, but also the Maryland Hall of Records. It introduced participants to archival theory and practice and the responsibilities of archival work through an intensive two-week program that concentrated on basic archival functions.

Other historic programs provided much needed help with inventorying and indexing local government records. The Works Progress Administration (WPA) was a New Deal agency from 1935 to 1943 that provided work relief for millions of jobless Americans. A sub-project, the Historical Records Survey (HRS), was originally a part of the Federal Writers' Project. Its goal of surveying and indexing historically significant records in state, county, and local archives was engendered in its mission statement, "the discovery, preservation, and listing of basic materials for research in the history of the United States."

It is no accident that the WPA instruction manual for preparing inventories of local archives was authored by T. R. Schellenberg. In many counties and municipalities in the United States, this project was the first time any sort of inventorying or systematic accounting of holdings was done. Guides to public and vital records, county archives inventories, and other finding guides were created throughout the country. Organized under the direction of future Librarian of Congress Luther H. Evans in 1935, it became part of the Work Projects Administration's Research and Records Program, Professional and Service Division in 1939. The groundbreaking program was terminated in 1943.

The Hoover Commission (1947), so named for its chair, former president Herbert Hoover, was charged with a massive reorganization of the federal government and to streamline many governmental practices. Among its major achievements was the introduction of systematic records management, to become what is now a part of the day-to-day functions of the National Archives. It also called for a Federal Records Act (1950), "to provide for the more effective creation, preservation, management, and disposal of records of the United States Government." This larger federal model had historic consequences for local governments since it provided a birth-to-death lifecycle framework for records created by departments and agencies not unlike those found on the local level.

The federal Freedom of Information Act (1966) and the Right to Privacy Act (1974) peripherally benefitted local government archives by promoting the notion of transparency in government. While these acts affected only federal records, they undoubtedly influenced states, and in turn, local governments, to acknowledge the rights of citizens to review government-created records. As state governments adopted open records laws, concepts of records management, the systematic retention and destruction of records, and the retention of permanently valuable records became inevitable and necessary services—whether properly funded or not.

Another program that impacted local government archives came in the form of the National Historical Publications and Records Commission (NHPRC) of the National Archives. Created in 1934 to fund the editing and publication of historical editions of the papers of prominent Americans, Congress expanded its mission over time to include funding for archival program planning and actual archival work. Since 1964, NHPRC has funded over four thousand two hundred projects, including many involving local government archives held by local governments, colleges and universities, libraries and historical societies, and other nonprofit organizations.[21]

Professional literature written specifically on or about local government records and archives practices is limited to only a few book-length treatments and a few dozen scholarly journal articles. *Local Government Records: An Introduction to Their Management, Preservation, and Use*, by former North Carolina state archivist H. G. Jones (1980), remains the only book solely devoted to managing archival materials in local governments. A cursory overview only, it is nonetheless an impassioned argument for the value of archives held within counties and municipalities. Bruce W. Dearstyne's *The Management of Local Government Records: A Guide for Local Officials* (1988) is the flipside of Jones's book, describing and outlining the best practices for records management in local governments. Its focus on active records disposition and non-permanent records, however, left little room for discussion of archives programs.

## INFLUENCE OF ARCHIVES AND RECORDS ORGANIZATIONS

In some cases, federal archives and records practices were adopted by state archives and historical societies, in turn providing models for local governments. While many aspects of local governments are funded by or mandated by the federal government, funding support for the preservation of permanent local government records has been historically limited. A steadying influence on the management of local government archives has been the organizations that helped define the archival and records management professions themselves. Perhaps the most significant organization to promote the creation and maintenance of local government archives programs is the Society of American Archivists (SAA). Founded in 1936, the Society of American Archivists is North America's oldest and largest national archival professional association. Prior to the Government Records Section and the Local Government Records Roundtable, the society sponsored a Municipal Records Committee, established in 1941, succeeded by a State and Local Records Committee in 1961. For several decades the committee encouraged and promoted best practices; perhaps its greatest achievement was a survey of records retention and disposition schedules in 1977.[22]

The influence of the records management field upon the direction of local government archives cannot be overstated, beginning with the Society of American Archivists' Records Management Committee, created in 1936 as the Reduction of Archival Materials Committee.[23]

One early organization that viewed the management of public records as a continuing, professional practice was the Public Administration Service (PAS). Chartered in 1933 in the State of Illinois to deliver professional management consulting and training to governmental and quasi-governmental departments and agencies, PAS originated in the 1930s. These services assisted local governments through problem solving and practical training. The organization served all levels of government in the United States, but always made local government development an important focus of its work.

ARMA International, established in 1955, is a nonprofit professional association for the records management field. In 1975, the Association of Records Executives and Administrators (AREA) and the American Records Management Association merged to form the present ARMA International. Its members include records managers, archivists, corporate librarians, legal professionals, information technology managers, and a wide variety of industries, in the United States, Canada, and many other countries. The association is known for its high level of organization and also develops and publishes standards and guidelines related to records management.[24] While its function is to facilitate and inform the professional about the broader field of records management, it has been an important ally in the preservation of records with permanent value.

Although SAA treated government records and archives as a primary area of interest for many years, it gradually became less of an advocate. The National Association of Government Archives and Records Administrators (NAGARA) was created in 1974 as a response to the Society of American Archivists' perceived indifference to government records and archives issues. More importantly, NAGARA's founders felt that the widening split between ARMA and SAA left a gap that could be filled by an organization where both archives and records management could be represented.[25]

There are now just over eighty-nine thousand local governments in the United States.[26] Some of these governments have active archives programs. Other permanently valuable local government records are under the care of historical societies and similar groups. But there are many more bodies of records languishing in unsuitable storage, under poor conditions for long-term preservation. Most of these places are also staffed by nonprofessionals, who cannot be faulted for lack of support or lack of experience. While there is a long and proud history of local archives programs, it is a sobering fact that the vast majority of local government archives do not have the support of their governments, in spite of their incalculable value and worth. Governments, individual employees, and responsible citizens must do whatever is within their means to protect and preserve these valuable assets of American history.

## NOTES

1. Dick Smith, "The Development of Local Government in Texas" (PhD dissertation, Harvard University, 1938).

2. "Great Britain has no general system of self-government. A certain number of cities and towns have been from time to time incorporated by the crown, or have successfully claimed the privilege as existing from time immemorial, either because in fact they have governed themselves from very ancient times, or because they have had such a representation in parliament as led to a presumption of their having been incorporated like the rest. The other urban districts have been regarded as mere 'upland towns' or populous townships, with nothing but a parochial organization, or the faint semblance of municipal institutions which grew out of the administration of fairs and markets." *Encyclopaedia Britannica*, 9th ed., s.v. "municipality," *Wikisource, The Free Library*, accessed July 29, 2012, http://en.wikisource.org/w/index.php?title=Encyclop%C3%A6dia_Britannica,_Ninth_Edition/Municipality&oldid=3973175.

3. Henry William Elson, *History of the United States of America* (New York: MacMillan, 1904), 210–16.

4. In the State of New York, the law creating the five boroughs is found in Chapter 378 of the *Laws of 1897*, and was called "The Charter of the City of New York." Though the term "borough" was not defined, per se, the law did state that the act provided "for the uniting into one municipality various communities, including the city and county of New York, the city of Brooklyn, the county of Kings, the county of Richmond, and part of the county of Queens with the municipal and public corporations therein." (Section 1620).

5. *Wikipedia*, s.v. "Poor relief," accessed September 11, 2012, http://en.wikipedia.org/w/index.php?title=Poor_relief&oldid=510353516; Sidney Webb, Beatrice Potter. *English Local Government from the Revolution to the Municipal Corporations* (London: Longmans, Green and Co., 1906).

6. "Parish Government Structure—The Forms of Parish Government," Police Jury Association of Louisiana, accessed May 20, 2013, http://www.lpgov.org/PageDisplay.asp?p1=3010.

7. "Parish Government Structure."

8. Dick Smith, "The Development of Local Government in Texas"; Bureau of Municipal Research, *Units of Local Government in Texas* (Municipal Studies No. 15) (Austin: Bureau of Municipal Research, University of Texas, 1941).

9. Geoffrey Pivateau, "Regidor," in *Handbook of Texas Online* (Austin: Texas State Historical Association), accessed July 21, 2012, http://www.tshaonline.org/handbook/online/articles/nfr01.

10. *Simon and Schuster's International Dictionary, English/Spanish, Spanish/English*, s.v. "legajo," (New York: Simon and Schuster, 1973), 1310.

11. League of Women Voters of California, *Guide to California Government*, 14th ed., (Sacramento: League of Women Voters of California Education Fund, 1992), chap. 16.

12. *Inventory of the County Archives of California: No. 41, San Luis Obispo County* (San Francisco: Northern California Historical Records Survey Project, 1939).

13. New Orleans Notarial Archives, accessed June 18, 2013, http://www.notarialarchives.org/history.htm.

14. *New York Local Government Handbook*, 6th ed. (Albany: New York State Department of State, 2011), 1–2.

15. Richard C. Berner, "Historical Development of Archival Theory and Practices in the United States," *Midwestern Archivist* 7, no. 2 (1982): 103–17.

16. Berner, "Historical Development of Archival Theory," 104.

17. David Levine, "The Management and Preservation of Local Public Records: Report of the State and Local Records Committee." *American Archivist* 40, no. 2 (1977): 190–99; Berner, "Historical Development of Archival Theory," 105–6.

18. "Emmet J. Leahy (1910–1964)," *Emmet J. Leahy Award*, accessed August 22, 2012 http://emmettleahyaward.org/leahy-bio.html.

19. *Philip C. Brooks Report, 1946–1950* (Austin: Dolph Briscoe Center for American History, University of Texas).

20. John H. Slate, "The Texas Library Association Archives and Local History Round Table 1950–2000: Fifty Years of Promoting the Role of Libraries In Preservation and Access to Primary Information," (Austin: Texas Library Association, 2000), 3.

21. NHPRC, http://www.archives.gov/nhprc/.

22. Finding Aid of the Society of American Archivists Records, University of Wisconsin–Milwaukee Libraries (undated); *Records Retention and Disposition Schedules: A Survey Report: A Project of the State and Local Records Committee of the Society of American Archivists* (Chicago: The Society of American Archivists, 1977).

23. Finding Aid of the *Society of American Archivists Records*.

24. *Wikipedia*, s.v. "ARMA International," accessed August 13, 2012, http://en.wikipedia.org/w/index.php?title=ARMA_International&oldid=420698220.

25. "A Brief History of NAGARA," NAGARA, accessed August 13, 2012, http://www.nagara.org/displaycommon.cfm?an=1.

26. "Census Bureau Reports There Are 89,004 Local Governments in the United States," U.S. Census Bureau, August 30, 2012, accessed August 7, 2014, http://www.census.gov/newsroom/releases/archives/governments/cb12-161.html.

# 2

---

# Types of Local Government Archives

Just as local governments operate in a wide variety of sizes and governing forms, so do local government archives operate in different offices and have a wide variety of records. Local government archives exist within municipalities and townships, counties and parishes, school districts, transportation authorities, and special authorities, such as public utilities and housing. The archives for these governing units function in a variety of ways. An archives might serve one of these types of governments, such as a county archives, or might be a centralized records agency for several different governments. For instance, a municipal archives might house not only the archival records of city departments, but also the records of the local transportation agency and the school system.

A local government archives might be one part of a larger records management function that also has oversight of non-permanent records, or an archives may be strictly devoted to permanent records and have no relationship to records management. The size and volume of holdings of local government archives can vary greatly and are not necessarily proportional to the size of the government. Regrettably, this is often due to indiscriminate destruction or the destruction of records by manmade and natural disasters such as fires, floods, and earthquakes. Some governments are very conscious of the permanent value of certain classes of documents, while others destroy materials believing they are irrelevant or waste valuable space.

## COMMON TYPES OF ARCHIVES

Municipal, town, and township archives comprise one of the most common types of local government archives. Organized archives and records centers for local governments are found throughout the United States in incorporated municipalities and serve both large and small cities. These governments may be several centuries old or may be ones that have functioned for only a few decades. While there are over eighty-nine thousand local governmental units in the country, only a fraction of them have formal archives programs.[1]

Municipal archives contain perhaps the widest variety of documents that can be found in one place. They touch on everything from the most specific matters (such as birth and death records and ordinances regarding personal behaviors and health) to general (such as sweeping laws concerning sanitation, traffic, and zoning). Virtually every facet of human and animal existence is regulated by some kind of law, which is reflected in the ordinances, resolutions, minutes, and collateral information generated by a governing body. Land transactions, construction, road building, water and wastewater, parks, libraries, and fire and police protection are just a few of the broad areas documented in a municipal archives.

County or parish archives may serve a few thousand residents or several million residents. The smallest county in the United States, Arlington County, Virginia, covers twenty-six square miles, while the largest is North Slope Borough, Alaska, covering over eighty-six thousand square miles. The population of counties varies from Loving County, Texas, with one hundred forty residents, to Los Angeles County, California, which is home to over nine million people.[2] In much of the United States, counties constitute the most important level of government. While all of these counties do not maintain an archives, they often create more permanent records than municipalities and other authorities and house more records with longer and permanent retention periods.

Documents relating to land sales, marriages, divorces, and some court records are created and maintained by county departments. Courts that hear felony cases and significant civil cases operate at the county government level in many states. Additionally, significant public activities, such as operating airports plus planning and zoning may be county activities. People are documented at the local level from birth to death and many significant events in between. As H. G. Jones commented in his book, *Local Government Records*, "The lesson is inescapable: county records in all but a few states constitute the most important documentation of the American past."[3]

Educating students is the primary duty of school districts, and the records of those students continue to be needed for many years after a student leaves the school system. Student records, along with information about alumni, are often found in school archives along with yearbooks, posters about special events, board minutes, photographs, copies of school newspapers, and other historical documentation. Individual students continue to need copies of their records as they return for additional schooling, while others use their transcripts to help prove identification. Current students, faculty, alumni, and area residents often use school archives to help instill pride in their respective institutions.

Public authorities are governmental or quasi-governmental entities having the responsibility of administering or operating something with public benefit, such as transportation districts, ports, hospitals, electricity, bodies of water, flood management, and public parks. They are often empowered to issue bonds to raise the capital necessary to build bridges, airports, railway lines, flood protection, and energy production and are subject to state and federal regulation, but—with few exceptions—are not subordinate to local governments.

Probably the most familiar public authorities are transportation related. Mass transit systems (airports, buses, railways, tollways, and turnpikes are examples), sometimes called intermodal transportation authorities, are self-governing corporations that fulfill the transit needs of a region and often overlay multiple local governments. For example, New York's Metropolitan Transportation Authority operates and regulates commuter rail, local and express buses, subways, and bus rapid transit, serving twelve counties in southeastern New York, along with two counties in southwestern Connecticut under contract to the Connecticut Department of Transportation.[4] Other examples include Bay Area Rapid Transit (BART), Dallas Area Rapid Transit (DART), and Washington Metro/Metrorail in Washington, D.C. Water-based transportation authorities include such agencies as the Port of Houston Authority and the Port of Los Angeles (whose formal name is the Los Angeles Harbor Department).

Other types of public authority archives maintain records about utilities such as electricity, natural gas, and water services. Examples can be found in cities and counties of all sizes and may be called a public utility district, or something more simplistic such as Memphis Light, Gas, and Water, the Los Angeles Department of Water and Power, or Cedar Falls (Iowa) Utilities. The permanent records of public authorities often include construction plans, board minutes, statistical information, photographs, and media coverage.

Counties, municipalities, and other local government entities create similar types of records, though they are seldom uniform in size, content, or value. Some basic records groups commonly found in many of these archives include minutes of the governing body, correspondence and subject files about projects undertaken by the government, maps and drawings, and select financial reports such as audits and budgets. Other kinds of historical files, such as newspaper clippings and photographs, are often found in all types of archives. Even with these commonalities, information may be stored in different formats, recorded in different ways, and called by different titles and even different departmental names. For example, one city's legal branch may be called a "municipal court," while another may be called the "corporation court." Regardless of name, however, all courts will have some sort of docket, which is the official schedule of proceedings in a court of law.

Some localities have lost vast amounts of their historic records in natural and man-made disasters (e.g., fire, flood, and vermin), while others have indiscriminately thrown out files over five or ten years old. Population size also makes a difference in the type and amount of records being created. Counties with a million residents produce a huge amount of records each year in comparison to those created by local governments with fewer than ten thousand people. A larger government is more likely to provide its residents more services than a smaller local government. The age of the governmental unit also makes a difference. Peachtree City, Georgia, a planned suburban municipality incorporated in 1959, has different types and relatively smaller amounts of records than a much older city, such as Charleston, South Carolina, which dates back to 1760.

## ARCHIVES AS ONE PART OF THE
## RECORDS KEEPING PROCESS

Decentralized local government archives, in which records are kept within the originating office, can be a simple and often inexpensive way of caring for government records. Records are sometimes kept in the office of a city or county clerk. In a small office, this approach relies on the record keeper to care for files throughout their lifecycle, from creation to disposal or permanent retention. The department or office-based approach presents an economical and effective way to establish both a records management and an archival program. Ideally a local government office will create and maintain records and use a state schedule, which is a document that identifies and describes an organization's records and provides instructions for the disposition of records throughout their life cycle. A schedule provides a timetable for how long a document must be kept; if a document is considered archival, it is retained permanently.

Departmental or office-based care of archival records works especially well for governments that create relatively few archival records, such as a small-town school board, small municipal government or individual offices within a county government (e.g., traffic or juvenile court). Economy and practicality are the biggest advantages of this system, which adds relatively little extra work to the operational costs of the office. Governments may want to store backup copies of records with state archives or in other secure places. Training personnel in record-keeping and archival practices poses the greatest expense, though many state and regional archives groups offer training to local officials at minimal costs.

The potential risk of decentralization is neglect. Even if an office of origin is charged with preserving its archival records, there is a very real possibility that some offices will ignore or flout ongoing maintenance. Another risk is that the records will receive no extra environmental protection. For example, heating and air conditioning may be turned off when offices are not occupied, or records may be stored in front of windows and subjected to light damage.

## ARCHIVES AS PART OF A GOVERNMENT RECORDS MANAGEMENT PROGRAM

A step beyond archival records being cared for in originating offices is an archival program integrated into a comprehensive local government records management program. In this instance, records are moved to a records center after they are no longer needed on a regular daily administrative basis. Some archival records, like deeds or minutes, may be kept for several years or permanently in the creating office. Upon receipt, records center staff place records slated for permanent retention in archival storage while records with temporary retention may be shelved in warehouse storage with less environmental control over heat and humidity. Vital materials and records that are expected to be heavily used or that have long retention periods or large annual accumulations may be scanned and kept in electronic format or microfilmed. In many municipalities and counties this includes such sizeable information as tax records and birth and death records. For more information on records management facilities, see the National Association of Government Archives and Records Administrators' local government records publication, *The Selection and Development of Local Government Records Storage Facilities.*

A combined records management and archives program is often the option of choice for governments that already have records management programs or that are establishing new records programs and want comprehensive records care in one central location under one program. Records center staff are usually trained to consider the entire life cycle of records and may only need additional archival and preservation training to handle archival records properly. Staff members should develop a historical perspective when dealing with archival records and understand that users of archival records may need a different level of assistance than internal records center users. Genealogists and local historians may be unfamiliar with older government record types and may require more specialized finding aids, access tools, or personal assistance than are usually found in a records center.

The main disadvantage of this system is that an archives might be designated as part of a records center in name only, without any real effort made to improve environmental controls or security. Upgrading storage areas to meet archival specifications may require additional expense and effort. Government administrators also may not fully appreciate the difference between records management and archives, or support the need for staff training in both aspects of records care. Continuing efforts may be necessary to fully educate local government funders and leaders about the importance of managing both inactive and archival records.

## STAND-ALONE ARCHIVAL PROGRAMS

Another option for a local government is to have an independent, stand-alone archival program that works with departments in the government which produce archival records. The archives might operate in its own building or in a dedicated space. It can be as minimal in activities or as complex as the institution is prepared to support. One program may operate a scanning unit which stores and retrieves information electronically, while another may operate on a very small budget and concentrate on the preservation of paper-based materials. There is no one correct model to follow.

One advantage of an independent archival program is that growth can be managed over time. An archives might start as a small center where a few records might be found. For instance, council minutes, newspapers, and photographs might be key archival holdings in the early stages. Later maps, building plans, and other materials may be incrementally added. Governments have permanent records that need to be kept in a safe and secure place. Having staff that can retrieve information as needed will allow the archives to prove its worth and value of the archives to government officials and area residents.

## MULTI-GOVERNMENT ARCHIVAL
## PROGRAMS (COOPERATIVE ARCHIVES)

Another configuration found in some parts of the United States is an archives that serves more than one local government. For some cities, counties, townships, and other forms of local government, it may be an economical alternative to pool resources. For a relatively small expense, governments can gain both the services of a trained archivist and archival storage of their historic records. Such a consortium may prove to be much more cost effective and practical than if a government developed its own archival program. Two such records programs have been operating in Georgia for over forty-five years combined: The Troup County Archives in West Georgia serves a population of sixty-four thousand and provides records management and archival services for the city of LaGrange, Troup County, and the Troup County Board of Education, while also operating a local history and genealogy library. The Thomaston-Upson County Archives in Middle Georgia serves twenty-seven thousand people and provides archival records care for cities in Upson County, Upson County's records, and those of the local board of education.[5]

Joint government archives programs often originate out of common needs. Frequently one government with records or an organization like a historical society will spearhead organizing efforts. Because different government records are living under one roof, it is common practice for the governments to formalize the relationship by ordinance or resolution, recognizing the singular archives as the official site for their records and empowering an administrator with the responsibility to care for the records. A resolution can give physical custody of the records to the archives but retain legal custody with the originating government.

A written agreement is usually negotiated about funding the archives. In different models, each government is charged a percentage of annual operating costs based on the total percentage of records stored in the archives; or on the amount of archival records produced annually by the government; or on the amount of use each government's records generate; or a combination of the three. For example, a county will probably have court, deed, marriage, and estate records, most of which require permanent retention. The county will have more archival records than other governments and would pay a higher percentage of costs for the archives. Alternatively, rates could be based largely on the number and amount of records pulled for researchers and government staff. Determining funding details early in the life of the archives is imperative and should be periodically reviewed.

A local cooperative archival program might provide reference services, preservation facilities, scanning and microfilming capability, and even records center services for non-permanent records. Such a local government archives is better accepted if it is located in a central place convenient to all the governments and their research base. A cooperative archives can be staffed by as few as one full-time and one part-time person, plus volunteers or interns who share duties on the reference desk. Such an archives provides an attractive option for local governments who want to keep their records nearby without the attendant space issues.

The greatest disadvantage to a cooperative archives is that archival records are physically removed from the creating office to an off-site storage facility. Local governments must ensure that state laws allow for records to be removed from their physical custody. In many states, records can be moved to designated centers, provided they are located within a certain number of miles of the main government office, or that the government has passed an ordinance permitting the physical relocation of records. In this business model, records of the different governments are kept distinct and separate. Records can be stored together physically, but kept apart under intellectual control. Access policies are a must to make provisions when governments want to see or borrow records they have relinquished to another repository.

## REGIONAL ARCHIVAL CENTERS

Yet another type of multi-government archival program is the regional archival center. Governments in several states have the option of placing their archival records in regional repositories operated by the state archives or by a regional government center. More times than not this type of institution is operated by a state archives. The representative is usually a professional archivist trained in the care of records. A regional center can be a great benefit for researchers who can use the records of a large geographic region at one location. Regional centers also help ensure proper care of records that a local government may not be able to accomplish. Regional representatives often become contact persons for local government officials when they have questions about records care.

The major problem with regional centers is that of other cooperative archives: records are geographically removed from the creating government. Some regions, especially in a sparsely populated area, may be quite large; regional centers may be many miles away from the creating governments and require long-distance travel to see the records.

One solution to the problem of decentralization is the regional historical resource depository (RHRD), which is found in just thirteen states, only nine of them active programs.[6] In the State of Texas, the state archives operates under Chapter 441.153, Subchapter J, of the Texas Government Code. Twenty-four depositories are located throughout the state in academic libraries and other institutions that meet criteria adopted by the Texas State Library and Archives Commission. Transfer of records is voluntary on the part of local governments, and each depository often has its own space limitations, so the volume and number of records series vary at each location.

## SENDING ARCHIVAL RECORDS TO A STATE ARCHIVES

A final decentralized model is for local governments to transfer archival records to the state archives. A local government may make exceptions to sending heavily used records, like deed books and marriage records, and may send digital or microfilm copies to the state archives. This approach works well for some states with smaller populations or smaller geographic areas. It provides a means of systematically documenting the activities of local governments throughout the state, and enables researchers to do their work at one site. Staff members at state archives have the expertise to care for records, and costs to local governments are usually minimal.

There are some disadvantages to state-facilitated care of local government records. A number of state archives in the mid-twentieth century over-committed services to local governments, only to be overwhelmed by the sheer volume of local records transferred. In the State of Georgia, a new State Archives building which opened in 1966 filled up within about twenty-five years. After reaching capacity, 159 counties in the state could only add microfilm of original records but not the physical records.

Even in smaller states, many separate governments create records. In some states, there is also territorial resentment regarding the state capital and state government. In other instances local governments may fear losing control of their records by turning them over to the state. Sending records to the state archives also increases travel from the local government to the state archives to see local records. Another disadvantage occurs when state governments endure budgetary crises and the archives is forced to cut back on reference service to researchers and service to local governments. Many state archives provide records schedules and guidance on records management and archival issues, but depend on local governments to take care of their own records.

## NOTES

1. U.S. Census Bureau, *2012 Census of Governments* (Washington, DC: U.S. Government Printing Office, 2012), accessed August 1, 2013, http://www.census .gov/govs/cog2012/.

2. "Counties," National Association of Counties, accessed August 1, 2013, http:// www.naco.org/Counties/Pages/default.aspx.

3. H. G. Jones, *Local Government Records: An Introduction to Their Management, Preservation, and Use* (Nashville, TN: American Association for State and Local History, 1980), 109.

4. "Metropolitan Transportation Authority (New York)," accessed July 24, 2014, http://en.wikipedia.org/wiki/Metropolitan_Transportation_Authority_%28New_ York%29.

5. "About Us," Troup County (Georgia) Archives, accessed July 28, 2014, http:// www.trouparchives.org/index.php/about_us; "History," Thomaston-Upson Archives, accessed July 28, 2014, http://www.upsoncountyga.org/tuarch/about/about.htm.

6. *The State of State Records, 2013 Edition: Statistical Report on State Archives and Records Management Programs in the United States* (Albany, NY: Council of State Archivists, 2013), 128.

# 3

## Local Government Archives and Records Management Programs

The fields of archives and records management share a number of common elements. A good working relationship with records management can present golden opportunities for a local government archives program that can pave the way for a lifetime of fruitful acquisitions. For those unfamiliar with the profession, records management is defined by Richard Pearce-Moses as "the systematic and administrative control of records throughout their life cycle to ensure efficiency and economy in their creation, use, handling, control, maintenance, and disposition."[1]

Most local governments are mandated by state law to operate some sort of records management, though the level of activity is often not dictated. Some governments have very robust programs, while others do only the minimal amount of work required by law to get by. Smaller governments often don't have budgets that can support both archives and records management so the responsibilities are sometimes combined. If you are primarily an archivist and you are assigned records management functions, it is a good idea to take advantage of educational opportunities wherever they arise. Conversely, if records management is your primary area of work and you have charge of the archival or permanent records as well, it behooves you to learn something about archives practices to gain an understanding of how these two areas of information science connect and interact.

Besides providing for the systematic disposal of unnecessary records, records schedules indicate what needs to be kept in an archives. Schedules can help identify records that may be missing from an existing archives holding. Some departments may be under the radar of the archives, or staff members may have assured archives employees that their records have no long-term value when they might actually need to be retained permanently.

There is a temptation to keep more than less, but there should be justification for what is kept. The fact is that only a fraction of local government records have enduring value. Author Bruce Dearstyne estimated in 1988 that less than 5 percent of local government records will have archival value based on their administrative, legal or historical use for the future.[2] An archivist should proceed judiciously when deciding to keep records longer than a stated retention period.

The decision making that follows is called appraisal. *Appraisal* is the process of determining the value and thus the disposition of the records based on legal requirements and current and potential long-term usefulness. One should consider both primary value of the record (why was it created) and secondary values (will people be using the records for other reasons?), as well as legal, fiscal, historical, and intrinsic values. For instance, a local government might have a storage room filled with fifty years of canceled checks and paid traffic tickets. Do they really need to be kept? Because the check or ticket is simply a record of a transaction (in both cases, the transfer of money), the informational value of that record declines dramatically in a short period of time. In reality, the odds of needing canceled checks more than two to five years old are exceedingly low. Therefore, if you have a schedule that provides an end date for their usefulness, you can legally and confidently dispose of the years of accumulation.

While this book cannot teach all of the fundamentals of records management, understanding retention schedules and how they work can be an invaluable tool for the local government archivist. Retention refers to how long public records need to be kept before destruction or transfer to an archives. Schedules document the common functions and activities of all the agencies within a local government, including administration of the agency and management of the agency's assets, finances, human resources, and information resources. Often other separate schedules relate to specific functions of the agency, such as public safety, health, courts, and public utilities.

## RECORDS RETENTION SCHEDULES

Records retention schedules are listings of records series commonly found in many divisions throughout a government. They describe the records of the organization and usually establish a projected timetable for the records, referred to as the life cycle of the record. Listings for individual records series may include various names for the records, a basic description, a recommendation for the minimum retention period, and citations for any legal retention requirements in federal, state, or local law. The schedules may include dispo-

Figure 3.1.   An employee in the records center of Clayton County, Georgia. Some archives programs are a part of or closely allied to records management programs. Image courtesy Clayton, County, GA. Photo by Kaye Lanning Minchew.

sition information of records, such as whether the records should be sent to the archives, or that they should be shredded after a specified date since they contain personal or sensitive information. Records schedules provide a basis for knowing what government records should be housed in the archives and are based on local, state, and federal regulations. Schedules properly adopted by the local government provide legal authority for disposing of some records while designating others as permanent records.

Archives employees or designated local government records staff should first consult schedules issued by their state archives or records center to determine which records merit permanent or long-term retention based on their administrative, fiscal, legal, informational, or evidential value. The state schedules specify the minimum amount of time that records are required to be kept; local governments may choose to keep certain records longer and the reasons should be documented on the inventory. In the example of a municipality updating its voting precincts, note that the records should be kept until after the next redistricting commission completes its work (usually this is done every ten years, based on the US Census) or a particular record series is retained permanently because of its historical value to the community.

## READING A RECORDS SCHEDULE

Records schedules can vary from place to place, but almost all have several common elements. The following table is adapted from the forms used by the State and Local Records Management division of the Texas State Library and Archives Commission:

The *Record Number* is a unique number that refers to a specific records series, such as "agendas" or "minutes" or "ordinances" or "resolutions." The number is usually assigned by the creator of the schedule. In the case of many local governments, the numbers are generated and assigned by the state library or state archives.

The *Record Title* is the name of the kind of record corresponding to the Record Number, usually referring to the type or function of the document—"charters," "correspondence" and so forth.

The *Record Description* is a more detailed explanation of the Record Title. Under the record title "Complaints," for example, the record description is "complaints received from the public by a governing body or any officer or employee of a local government relating to government policy." The expanded description helps records and archives specialists define and understand what records fit within which series.

The *Retention Period* is the length of time the document(s) must be kept. Retention periods are either permanent or temporary. Permanent records are, by definition, suitable for transfer to archives. An example of a temporary retention period for a series titled "Contracts," might be "X years after the expiration or termination of the instrument." For a series titled "Public Relations Records," the official retention period might be two years, but if deemed valuable to the archives, can be changed to permanent.

In the retention period notes, abbreviations are frequently used and include such retention periods as:

AV—As long as administratively valuable
FE—Fiscal year end
AC—Administrative Code

**Table 3.1.**

| Record Number | Record Title | Record Description | Retention Period | Remarks |
|---|---|---|---|---|
| GR1000-03a | MINUTES | | | |
| GR1000-08 | SPEECHES, PAPERS, AND PRESENTATIONS— ELECTED OFFICIALS | Written minutes. Notes or text of speeches, papers, presentations, or reports delivered in conjunction with government work by elected officials. | PERMANENT. End of term in office or termination of service in that position. | Retention Notes: a) For speeches, papers, and presentations of other local government staff see GR1000-51. b) Review before disposal; some records may merit PERMANENT retention for historical reasons. |
| GR1000-45 | CALENDARS, APPOINTMENT AND ITINERARY RECORDS | Calendars, appointment books, or programs, and scheduling or itinerary records, purchased with local government funds or maintained by staff during business hours that document appointments, itineraries, and other activities of agency officials or employees. | CE + 1 year. | Retention Note: A record of this type purchased with personal funds, but used by a public official or employee to document his or her work activities may be a local government record and subject to this retention period. See Open Records Decision 635 issued in December 1995 by the Texas Attorney General. |
| *GR1000-05 | ORDINANCES, ORDERS, AND RESOLUTIONS | | PERMANENT. | Retention Note: Includes ordinances, orders, or resolutions that have been repealed, revoked, or amended. |

US—Until superseded
LA—Life of asset
CE—Calendar year end

Most of the abbreviations are self-explanatory. The "Administrative Code" designation refers to the local administrative code used by your local government. This is the City Code or the Municipal Code of Civil and Criminal Ordinances or a county code. "Life of asset" refers mostly to equipment or vehicles owned by a government. For instance, the records kept on a police vehicle are eligible for destruction once the vehicle becomes unusable or is decommissioned from service.

The *Remarks* field is where special notes are made about series which might not be so cut and dried. Under the series titled "Personnel Studies and Surveys," the retention period may be stated to be three years, though the remarks field could include a note like, "Review before disposal; some documents may merit PERMANENT retention for historical reasons."

## COMMON RECORDS SERIES

Most states issue schedules for records common to all local governments, frequently called the Local Schedules. Common records of local governments include minutes of meetings of the governing body, land records, court records, publications, early government records, audits, legal opinions, architectural materials, and photographs and other graphic and audio materials. Among those usually found in most states are:

Records of County Clerks
Records of District Clerks
Records of Elections and Voter Registration
Records of Public Health Agencies
Records of Justice and Municipal Courts
Records of Public Safety Agencies
Records of Public Works and Other Governmental Services
Records of Property Taxation

## TYPES OF RECORDS FOUND IN LOCAL GOVERNMENT SERIES

Many different types of documents are found within records series. *Minutes* are generally written proceedings of a body of the government or of government boards or commissions that address specific subjects. The minutes are usually approved at future meetings and are often the single most important body of records that a local government will house. A wide variety of information can be found in minutes, ranging from acceptance of a state or federal government grant to a resolution passed on the death of a governing body member. Other minutes might reference agreements used to build major highways, or actions taken to conserve water or build lakes to improve irrigation water for farms.

*Legal records* include opinions and interpretations of existing laws and regulations and should be retained for both internal and external users. The opinions may relate to interpretations of new state or federal regulations. Especially in the Southern United States, files created by city, county, and district attorneys during the Civil Rights era will be of long-term historical interest. Other legal files of a more temporary nature should be retained according to the schedules. These files can include lawsuits filed by citizens for injuries on city property, as well as lawsuits against law enforcement for unlawful arrest. When deciding about legal files, remember that court dockets and court cases may already include basic information; attorney files should generally be retained only if they add information and details to the case.

Another sort of legal record, *court documents*, also has important permanent value. These files can include divorce records and criminal and civil cases. Divorce records can shed light on trends in causes for termination. Criminal files might detail sensational murders as well as lesser transgressions. Antebellum records in former slave-holding states provide invaluable insights into runaway slaves and perspectives of the institution of slavery as a business.

*Financial records* of enduring value include budgets and audits that indicate spending priorities of governments. Audits often reveal the effectiveness or ineffectiveness of government programs. Findings of audits may lead to policy changes or may be early indicators of serious trouble in a government. Budgets will reflect hard economic times—they may show cuts in funds for personnel or public works. During recessions, these accounts may reveal the kinds of budget cuts required to keep the government afloat. Financial records can also reflect changes in social attitudes and mirror the prevailing political party of the time. Audit reports can also refute media. Newspaper stories may tell one story when actual data tells another story. Financial reports that recommend changes in policies and procedures are particularly important, especially when these findings result in actual change in business practices.

*Official publications* of municipalities and counties have enduring value and in some cases have operational value as vital documents. This includes traditional print media such as flyers, brochures, pamphlets, and studies and reports prepared by both staff and outside advisors or consultants, but also electronic publications such as websites and social media. Governments produce a wide variety of publications, from ephemera such as employee newsletters, posters, and pamphlets to the more essential charters and codes that are periodically published for municipalities and counties.

*Codes* are particularly important to collect and save since they are a snapshot of the laws regulating the government at a specific time and often include vital information on ordinances adopted by the government that may or may not still be in effect. Civil, criminal, fire, construction and other codes detail regulations affecting such things as public behavior, construction standards, planned developments, and zoning. Superseded codes from the past are among the most heavily used materials in local government archives, frequently requested by internal users for the protection of government assets, and by external users for legal defense and relief. Codes are also useful sources of outdated or superfluous laws. This includes amusing and quaint offenses, such as spitting on sidewalks, loose livestock on property, and failing to doff hats to females. More serious examples of outdated laws include racial segregation regulations of business; personal conduct; neighborhoods; housing; public transportation; educational facilities; and city facilities such as parks, playgrounds, and pools. No matter the part of the country, laws from the era of segregation are a very important resource for learning about day-to-day lives of people of color.

*Public relations/public information materials* including press releases, speeches by mayors or governing body members, and position papers on local issues can reveal much about the operations and priorities of a government. The materials may relate to specific programs or they may be aimed at issues of the day. Other public relations materials document how governments will react to public safety issues such as natural disasters and civil disturbances. Local governments in coastal or tornado-prone areas, for example, will issue emergency information about what residents should expect during a hurricane or evacuation information.

Land and land development records can be extremely valuable in documenting the growth and expansion of a city or county. Subdivision plans, zoning materials, street and highway development, and corporate boundaries files have permanent administrative, legal, and historical value. Materials documenting a boundary dispute with a neighboring city, county, or state can be most informative if the files explain the history of how and where a boundary is set. When money is at stake, land records become valuable exhibits in litigation for both sides.

An example from the state of Georgia illustrates the value of these records. A dispute between a city-county government and a neighboring county over the land where a major shopping area was being developed required a ruling

## City Assisted Evacuation Plan (CAEP)

A Guide to
Accessing the CAEP

ONE
NEW ORLEANS
Rethink • Renew • Revive
C. Ray Nagin, Mayor

### What is the CAEP?

The City-Assisted Evacuation Plan (CAEP) is a program designed to help people who have no means of evacuating on their own. This may be due to financial need, unreliable or no transportation, or homelessness. If you feel you may be eligible for the CAEP, call the City's 311 hotline or the 800 numbers listed on the back of this brochure and answer the phone survey. If you are eligible for the CAEP, you will be notified via postcard and your information kept in a database for registration during evacuation.

#### Important information for CAEP Users:

• If any information changes after you have registered, please call 311 to update these changes.

• Bring identification with you when you evacuate including State-issued license or ID card. If you do not have any documentation, you will NOT be turned away.

• Bring only 1 small carry-on bag per person (no more than 45" total dimensions). Pet carriers, purses, and diaper bags will not count as your one bag.

• Bring your medicines and prescriptions (must be in their original bottles or packages).

• Bring important papers for safekeeping.

• Bring cash with you. Banks at evacuation locations may be unable to process debit or credit cards. Bring a book of checks to use.

• Those with special medical physical or psychological needs should consult physicians, counselors, home health care agencies, and service providers to arrange care where they are going.

• The elderly, mobility-impaired and those that need medical resources should go to a CAEP senior center for evacuation pickup. These have mobility access and are staffed to assist people with non-routine concerns. All others should report to a general pickup point listed inside.

• Those transported to special needs shelters will only be allowed to bring one caretaker with them.

• If you bring a pet during CAEP, it must have ID, collar, leash, be up to date on vaccines, and have any needed medications.

• *NO WEAPONS, ALCOHOL, OR DRUGS WILL BE ALLOWED. ALL SUCH ITEMS WILL BE CONFISCATED.*

For more information on the CAEP or emergency planning:
311
1-877-286-6431
1-800-981-NOLA (TTY)
www.nolaready.com

To register for the city emergency alert system:
www.nolaready.info

EMERGENCY
or
Ptext message NOLA4US

---

**Figure 3.2.** A post–Hurricane Katrina brochure from the papers of New Orleans Mayor Ray Nagin. Ephemera, or items meant to serve only an immediate purpose, often provide a wealth of information about historic events and places. Image courtesy Louisiana Division/City Archives, New Orleans Public Library.

by the Georgia secretary of state. Both counties wanted the property and sales tax monies generated by the new businesses. Because of careful research, one government was able to stake a stronger claim to the tax revenue. Land and development records are of great interest for legal reasons (when and how did the changes happen?), administrative reasons (are taxes being paid to the proper authorities?) and historical reasons (documentation of acres of farm land transformed into shops, restaurants, and parking lots) as the character of an area changes.

Similarly, deeds are very valuable. Deeds indicate when pieces of property are bought and sold. They are often filed at the county level, but can be found in a city if the documents involve public land that is part of a municipality. Such records can indicate the economic status of an area and property changes and pricing, and they can help governments decide if zoning and other land regulation needs to be implemented.

Deeds are also often used in title searches and in genealogical research. Knowing where ancestors lived and who neighbors were can explain much about family history. Documenting where families lived can indicate relationships and explain migration, as families may have joined together to travel before settling new communities. Deed transactions might also reveal information about the postwar migration of African Americans from the South to cities in the North.

*Subject files and case studies* on topics like public education or strategies in dealing with law enforcement issues can show how thinking and dealing with such topics by governments and society change over time. For instance, studies reflect the way police or sheriffs' departments confront issues of drugs or gangs in their cities and counties over time and evolve over the decades. These files often document changes in major policies and procedures. They may also document individual neighborhoods and communities. Files about the development of a water authority in a rural area may be the earliest indications of the development of a new incorporation. Other files about controversial issues may reflect the prevailing attitudes of government officials and can document changes in such areas as race, ethnicity, and gender.

*Maps* are invaluable tools in archives research. They reflect changes brought by new roads and streets, housing, or commercial developments around major thoroughfares and interchanges. Other maps may show massive geographic changes that affect an area when lakes, reservoirs, and levee systems are built. Maps provide evidence of roads moved or obliterated, and routes of travel that have changed over time.

*Marriage, birth, and death* records are considered vital records and are recorded at the local level—usually with the county, sometimes in municipalities, and occasionally both. States usually retain copies of birth and death records as well. While some archives are willing to take on the task of providing access to these heavily requested documents, others decline because of traffic volume or the added responsibility of adding certification or other official validation.

Vital records help people document their identity and possible name changes. For family historians, marriage records can provide important documentation about individuals. Over time, marriage records reveal changes in how society views relations between different races and sexual orientation. For instance, up until the mid-1960s, some cities, especially in the Deep South, maintained separate sets of marriage books for whites and blacks. Practices evolve with the legal and societal acceptance of marriages between people of different races and same genders.

The records of *school systems and school districts* include administrative records such as minutes of school board meetings and legal opinions, which are important archival records created at the higher decision-making level. Maps showing changes in school districts can be extremely valuable, not only for the primary reason for which they were created (to show families where their children should go to school), but also because the maps have secondary values demonstrating population growth and geographic changes. School census records of the nineteenth century are often used by genealogists and can show migration patterns of ethnic groups across the country.

Other permanent archival records found in school systems include internal reports and studies; deeds; graduation and class-ranking lists; school census data; and teacher, parent, and student handbooks. Histories about schools and school systems and student annuals (yearbooks) constitute other popular archival records worth preserving.

For some systems, school consolidations and mergers between neighboring districts can signal the first steps toward later consolidations of city and county governments or may simply signal the end of historic rivalries when two or three schools merge into a larger school.

School district records should be carefully reviewed for records that document the history of segregation, as well as the history of integration, one of the most fundamental changes in American society. The slow merging of white and black schools into one following the U.S. Supreme Court's 1954 *Brown vs. Board of Education* rulings occurred over about twenty years and is represented in district law enforcement files, court-mandated busing reports and records, and of course in administrative records.

## RECORDS OF SPECIAL PURPOSE DISTRICTS AND QUASI-GOVERNMENTAL ENTITIES

Special purpose districts are established to perform specific functions locally, independent of municipal or county governments. These districts include transportation authorities for airports, ports, highways, and mass transit, and also for such things as land appraisal, fire protection, libraries, parks, cemeteries, hospitals, irrigation, conservation, sewerage, solid waste, stadiums, water supplies, electric power, and natural gas utilities.[3] While they are subject to local, state, and federal regulations to operate, they are in effect local governments with their own governing bodies, police and fire departments, and other offices. Each may have their own idiosyncratic record-keeping practices, but it is still helpful to think of districts and authorities as a specialized form of local government.

Two examples of independent quasi-governmental agencies are the Dallas–Fort Worth International Airport and the Chicago Transit Authority. The Dallas–Fort Worth International Airport is governed by a board of directors composed of twelve members, eleven of whom are appointed by the city councils of the airport's owner cities. Seven represent the City of Dallas and four represent the City of Fort Worth. A twelfth, nonvoting board position represents one of the airport's four neighboring cities. The Chicago Transit Authority's governing body is the Chicago Transit Board, which consists of seven members, four appointed by the mayor of Chicago and three appointed by the governor of Illinois.

Records series of *utility services* having permanent value often include maps and plats, planning studies and reports, rate scheduling documentation, operations records, publications, and interactions with regulatory authorities, among other subjects. Series of *transportation authorities* to consider for the archives include, but are not limited to, charters and bylaws, meeting minutes and agendas, jurisdictional boundary documentation, legal opinions, publications, press releases and community relations records, contracts, and planning and studies materials. These are only a few examples of the kinds of documents encountered in special purpose districts.

## OTHER ISSUES RELATING TO ARCHIVES
## AND RECORDS MANAGEMENT PROGRAMS

What is perhaps most important for an archivist to know about records series in records management applications is that whatever they are called, the title must be descriptive of the nature of the materials. Nonsense titles like "Miscellaneous Papers" and "General Information" should be avoided because they do not tell anyone what the records actually are, or what they are about. An archivist should always find a way to meaningfully describe groupings of records and documents. Don't try to reinvent the wheel; state-issued schedules for local governments across the country include many useful examples of what to title a records series.

Many states recommend that early local government records be kept permanently regardless of their subject matter, especially if it appears there is often no other source for the information. If the locality did not have a newspaper, or if fire or floods have destroyed other local resources, government sources may be wholly unique and invaluable. Collecting cutoff dates and ranges are set individually from repository to repository, though it is frequently recommended that all records dating before 1900 are retained permanently. Because local governments are fluid entities that are continually producing records, many archives collect current records alongside much older ones.

What would you do if you had dozens of cubic feet of water bills from 1915? You might just keep a few as examples. Sampling records is another solution for records that have little informational value but do have intrinsic value if they illustrate a unique method or format of business from an older time period.

## USING RECORDS MANAGEMENT
## SCHEDULES FOR APPRAISAL

The permanent value of certain record groups is self-evident, such as ordinances, minutes of public meetings, or land and probate records. Written or typed minutes, particularly, are usually considered the official permanent record of a meeting, trumping other media such as audio or video recordings. Alternatively, archivists and even researchers may see worth in records whose values are not so apparent.

Because schedules determine when a record's original life cycle is concluded, it is essential for the archivist to be actively involved in the disposition process. In an ideal setting, records management staff who are trained to flag materials from a certain time period will alert archives staff to review the boxes during the authorization for disposal process. If deemed worthy of transfer, the disposition of the boxes is noted on the authorization form and transferred formally to the permanent custody of the archives.

When appraising records that might have permanent worth, consider whether the records contain significant information about persons, places, events, or corporate bodies and their value for research. Local records provide insights into local customs, prevailing attitudes toward gender and race, historical time periods, and social mores that may be hard to find in other types of documents. For example, local county court minutes may reveal anything from fines levied for poor manners in front of women, to the making of illegal liquor during Prohibition, to community moral standards regarding the 1970s fad of "streaking."

Government records inform interdisciplinary fields such as social science, environmental studies, city and urban planning, history, the arts, medicine, genealogy and family history (informational value), as well as documents that contain evidence of the government's origins, functions, and activities (evidential value). In the appraisal process to determine archival value, the archives employee or designated local government records employee should not only consult common retention schedules, but also revisit and evaluate its administrative, fiscal, legal, informational, or evidential value.

It is sometimes just as valuable to pay attention to the dates of a records series as content. The value of a record may relate to external circumstances beyond its informational content such as scarcity, format, or creator. In the case of mass destruction (such as fire or flood), in which records of other businesses in a locality are destroyed, even examples of letterheads can increase in importance.

Just because you *can* save it doesn't mean you *should*. Before deciding to keep records that are not designated for long-term retention permanently, one should weigh the cost to taxpayers of long-term retention against possible use. In the case of voluminous records such as tax rolls and twentieth-century records, consider keeping a small sampling—perhaps 1–5 percent of the files every year—or possibly keep one year of records for every five or ten years. Another alternative would be to keep all of the records for a few early years. In spite of low research value, traffic tickets from the first years that automobiles arrived in a town can be of interest to the general public, as would a listing of early tag numbers.

When retaining records beyond their retention date, you should have good reasons to explain why they should be kept. Notes might designate permanent value because of a series' historical value to the community or because of interest in a specific event, group, or person. While it is unlikely that you'll need to contact citizens for input, it is good to remember that that option is available. The National Archives occasionally notifies and requests input from the public during the review process of records that can have unusual interest or research value.[4]

## THE DISPOSITION AND DISPOSAL PROCESS

Once records have reached the end of their retention period, it is time to initiate the disposal process for documents that have reached, or will reach, the end of their lifespan. In all established records management programs there is a procedure for gaining the proper permissions for disposal, sometimes referred to as an Authorization for Records Disposal, Disposal Authorization, Records Disposal Authority, or similar name. The authorization is also used to track and report on the volume and kinds of records discarded. The disposal process is an important tool for identifying potential additions to the archives because it provides an opportunity for the records management staff to alert the archives staff to items that might otherwise fall through the cracks.

Records management practices can be strict when defining what is a local government record and what is a "non-record." Such non-records include duplicates, clippings from newspapers, magazines, and journals. It is up to the archivist to determine if these should be retained permanently. While these files are not official records of the local government, they provide valuable insight into the events or topics addressed by the local government. This series can include television and radio reports and programs on audio and video media.

Such files may include reports from council meetings, and updates on proposed new programs such as a water or sewer system expansion. Clippings can also cover historical topics such as reports by the police department of the City of Dallas following the assassination of President John F. Kennedy or the official position of a California municipality regarding water-saving programs during times of severe droughts. Other clippings might result when a government hosts or cosponsors major events, such as marathons. The tragedies of the bombings at the Murrah Federal Building in Oklahoma City in 1995 and the Boston Marathon of 2013 yielded countless stories across the city, state, nation, and world. Because so many municipal agencies and departments were involved in the events and their aftermath, saving these non-records have a connection to municipal and county departmental records with safety and law enforcement agencies. Similarly, changes in safety procedures for buildings and events should be saved and documented.

## NOTES

1. Richard Pearce-Moses, "Records Management," in *A Glossary of Archival and Records Terminology* (Chicago: Society of American Archivists, 2005), accessed August 14, 2015, http://www2.archivists.org/glossary.

2. Bruce Dearstyne, *The Management of Local Government Records* (Nashville, TN: American Association of State and Local History,1988), 39.

3. U.S. Census Bureau, *2002 Census of Governments, Vol 1, Number 1, Government Organization* (Washington, DC: U.S. Government Printing Office, 2002), vii–viii.

4. National Archives and Records Administration (NARA), *Records Schedule Review Process*, accessed August 25, 2015, http://www.archives.gov/records-mgmt/policy/records-schedule-review-process.html.

# 4

# Establishing and Planning Local Government Archives Programs

While all local governments have records of enduring value, not all have formal archives programs. Whether you are in charge of thousands of feet of records, or have a more modest amount, there are a host of things that should be considered in preparation for opening an archives. Setting up an archives, either by itself or connected to a records management program, does not have to be a daunting task. With careful planning and leverage of resources, even the most cash-strapped local government can establish good practices and institute basic preservation principles that can achieve the most basic goals of an archives—preservation and access.

When using the phrase "archives program," we mean a formal activity that operates by virtue of some kind of authority—whether codified in a local government code or not. Support from top management is essential to success. Some archives have come to exist by the simplest and most organic means, by merely surviving and accumulating. A closet full of boxes or a basement full of ledgers may be called "the archives" by staff members and be regarded with some words of respect, but such words do not equate to a planned and managed program of action. Having a genuine functioning program is important for a number of reasons, especially when an archives seeks grant funding for records projects. *It is not enough to simply say you have an archives*. Most archives have some level of staffing, are open to the public for so many days per week or month, and have policies governing their operation and use.

In some cases, archives programs have their origin in pending anniversaries or historical milestones. While these can be a great impetus to generate interest in creating an archives, be wary of their intentions and sustainability. An archives program should be more than designating a space and filling it with boxes for the sake of marking a significant milestone or anniversary. Too often after the celebration the "archives" are neglected and forgotten, languishing in a setting that may not be much better than where they were previously found.

It is important first and foremost to understand where a local government archives program fits into the government's hierarchy. Would there be an advantage to being a stand-alone operation, or is it better to be a subordinate part of a department? Even if this is a decision that is out of the archivist's hands, it is nonetheless valuable to know where you fit within the larger organization.

Many programs are a division or part of a county or municipal clerk or city secretary, but can also be under the direct authority of a city manager, the city council, or in a county, under a county's commissioners or other governing body. When considering the formation of a formal archives program, one of the first questions to consider is which department or unit of local government is best equipped and most logical to administer a program. The effectiveness and sustainability of an archives depends greatly upon where it is quartered, where the administrative charge for the program lies, and how that administrative charge is written.

Local government archives are most commonly located within the office of a city clerk or city secretary, or a county clerk or county administrator. This is usually because these offices are considered the official record keeper of the government. Their authority to administer and manage vital records is sometimes written into the government's code of regulatory ordinances. The reach or extent of authority, however, depends upon the strength of the ordinance.

Archives can function well in many different environments that are

- in a separate department offering both records management and archival services;
- in an area resource center to provide archival services—and also perhaps records management services—to two or more local governments forming a local consortium where governments join together to support an archives;
- functioning as part of a regional repository operated by state archives or by a region;
- located in a state archives and receiving records from local governments around the state.

Each of these approaches has features suited to different types of government and political climates. Across the nation, programs of each type exist and operate well within their governments. At times, an archival program grows into a different type of archives as user needs change.

There is no single model for a local government archives. In some very large local government entities an archives may be a part of a division of vital records or a department of records, as is the case in New York City and Philadelphia. Other local government archives are located within state government–administered settings, such as Maryland's Hall of Records or the Regional Depository Program of the Texas State Library and Archives Commission. In some cities and counties, the special collections unit of the local public library may serve as a de facto archives. Still other configurations include government records under the care of a local historical society or a nonprofit local history organization. What is important to monitor and enforce in all of these arrangements is that they have written authority to exist and be accessible to users.

Local and state laws regarding local government records must be adhered to, including compliance with laws regarding open records. Also, many states have laws that prohibit public records from being held by private entities without express permission of the creating entity. One exception would be a local government that no longer exists, such as a town consumed through annexation or consolidation. Other laws that apply to public records, such as privacy laws, will most likely still apply to records regardless of age. It is good to be aware of the variety of information that is contained within the records of your archives.

## ARCHIVES WITHIN RECORDS MANAGEMENT PROGRAMS

In its most ideal setting, a local government archives is a part of a records management program or office, or at least connected administratively. Because properly implemented records management programs are established through legal authority, the systematic disposition of records becomes an active, even aggressive process by which documents having permanent value are more easily and systematically identified. In other words, it is an organic conduit for archival records and there is less opportunity for high-value records to slip through the cracks.

Furthermore, archives programs and records management programs support each other. An archives program is stronger and less likely to be defunded when supported by an existing records management program. The presence of sound records management discourages negligent and thoughtless destruction of records and encourages the systematic preservation of worthy materials. In more cases than can be related, historically valuable materials were identified and rescued through the orderly and methodical authorization for disposal process.

Records management law is now a reality in all fifty states and the territories of the United States. In state government–based programs, the state identifies common records series and helps local governments develop processes to efficiently manage their records. Instead of having to create schedules from scratch, local governments can use and refine them to fit their needs. Understanding what can and cannot be disposed of legally is an important foundation for an archives program.

A records management ordinance is often the best place to codify and outline the charges of an archivist or an archives program. It not only must outline the duties of the records manager or administrator, but should include provisions for the preservation of historic or permanently valuable physical and digital records. Some records management ordinances establish a records management committee for final permissions for disposition. Make every effort to ensure an archivist is made a permanent member of the committee.

The body of the ordinance needs to define the responsibilities of departments, department heads, and departmental records liaisons with respect to the care and disposition of permanent records, defining ownership of local government records, and adopting records control schedules for the legal and efficient disposal of records no longer having permanent value, as well as directing records of enduring value to be placed in the government archives. Because so many programs are focused primarily on paper records, it is essential to include a statement that requires the local government to manage digital records.

While it is not necessary to physically designate a location for a records center and archives within the ordinance, it is important to establish both in name for reasons of permanency. Once the ordinance is passed by the local government, it will be required to provide some kind of space for these operations.

## PLANNING AN ARCHIVES

There are a number of issues to consider when planning an archives program. One example is acquisition scope. Would you acquire only the products of the day-to-day decision making of elected officials—ordinances, resolutions, and minutes—or would you also collect their correspondence? The collecting scope of the program can be shaped by such things as what is being collected at other local or regional institutions, and definitions of what is considered a government record or document. Collecting scope or collecting guidelines should be written and approved by top management, preferably in the codified directive establishing the archives. A mission statement is another formal document that can outline the kinds of materials you will or will not accept.

Other important things to plan for include the administrative authority of the archives (who reports to whom?); physical space and storage considerations (including growth space); staffing; and, perhaps most importantly, determining the source of ongoing support (will the local government make a long-term or permanent commitment to funding an archives program?). Many of these issues are addressed in great detail in such publications as *Keeping Archives*, by the Australian Society of Archivists (2008) and Elizabeth Yakel's *Starting an Archives* (1994).

The most sound foundation for a local government archives is one that has the authority to operate by legal mandate. This could mean being codified in the charter of a city or governmental entity, or charged with responsibilities through an ordinance or law passed by a local government elective body. It is most advantageous if an archives program can be clearly identified as a part of a records management program, though this is not always possible. Whatever the arrangement, legal authority to exist and operate can prevent defunding and neglect, as well as demonstrate to a government the value of preserving and making accessible its institutional history.

The cities of Seattle, Washington, and Dallas, Texas, offer two examples of enabling legislation and authority in a local government. Both archives programs' legislations are reproduced in entirety in appendix A. In Seattle, the archives program was established in 1984, separately from the records management program, which was implemented in 2002. An ordinance passed by its city council in 2013 joined the two in a single program, which cemented their administration under one department.

In the Seattle ordinance, the language includes prefatory matter, a set of definitions, administrative responsibilities, the scope of work of the archives, responsibilities of elected officials and administrative staff, care of archival records, certification of reproductions for legal admissibility, and public access conditions. In this last section, it is important to be clear that all records in the archives are open for unfettered use and cannot be restricted, unless there is a compelling legal exemption.[1]

The authorization for the Dallas Municipal Archives to operate as the repository for the permanent records of the City of Dallas is contained within Chapter 39C of the Dallas City Code of Civil and Criminal Ordinances, the city's records management program. The program enumerates such fundamental concepts of archives and records management as definitions, ownership and custody, disposition of records, and duties and responsibilities of various governmental parties. Subsection 17 of that chapter then outlines the responsibility of the archives as follows:

SEC. 39C-17. DALLAS MUNICIPAL ARCHIVES AND RECORDS CENTER.
(a) The Dallas municipal archives and records center (DMARC) serves as a centralized records storage facility for all departments for the storage of noncurrent city records. DMARC also serves as *the repository for permanent and historical city records that are transferred to the facility by departments.*
(b) DMARC is under the direct control and supervision of the records management officer. The records management officer shall establish policies and procedures regulating the operations and use of DMARC by city departments. (Ord. Nos. 20787; 23267)[2]

An example of enabling legislation for a county archives and records program is found in the Multnomah County Code for Multnomah County, Oregon:

§ 8.501 POLICY.
It is the policy of the County to maintain a professional archives and records management program consistent with state law and with current archives and records management professional standards.
§ 8.502 ADMINISTRATION.
(A) This subchapter shall be administered by the Records Management and Archives Program. A County Records Officer shall be appointed by the Department to coordinate the records management program and to serve as liaison with the State Archivist as required by ORS 192.105(2)(a).
(B) The Records Management and Archives Program shall develop Administrative Rules as necessary:
(1) To provide for the orderly management, maintenance and care of County records consistent with State public records laws and rules promulgated by the State Archivist;
(2) To provide for the transfer of custody of all County archival records to the Records Management and Archives Program at such time as a department determines that the department does not have an operational need for the records; and
(3) To identify and preserve County archival records.[3]

Another crucial tool in the establishment of a solid archives program is a mission statement or similar type of declaration that identifies essential functions and the scope of work. A mission statement is valuable because it can say as much about what an archives *does not* do as what it *does*. For instance, Rutherford County, Tennessee's mission statement is simple and to the point:

The Rutherford County Archives seeks to preserve and protect the written documents, past and present, generated by the government offices of Rutherford

County, TN. The county records preserved at the archive include judicial proceedings, tax documents, and administrative records. The preservation of most of these records is required by law and serves to protect the rights of citizens. The Rutherford County Archives seeks to make these documents accessible to government agencies, the people of Rutherford County, and the public at large."[4]

When considering the kind of archives to establish, a local government should decide what kind of program will work best in the current situation. Some programs evolve over time as needs change. An inter-office program where the same staff create, maintain, and dispose of records or transfer into an archives can grow into a larger records management and archival program, which might evolve into a regional archival center. Alternatively, a local government that sends all of its records to the state archives or a regional center might later decide they need to have digital images or microfilm copies of their archival records and set up an archival information room at the local government building.

It is worth noting that some local government archives programs may be established years after another department or governmental unit has been collecting similar materials. An example would be a municipal library with a special collections unit; a government-funded museum is another example. In both these cases, archival materials can be repatriated to the new archives, though it may be easier and in the government's best interests to leave it be. As long as the records are being well cared for and accessible within another department, it may not be worth the trouble to transfer.

## JUSTIFICATION FOR AN ARCHIVES PROGRAM

There are many issues to consider besides deciding what kind of archives to have. These include funding, staffing, and space/building requirements. Invariably, after the archives is proposed, the first question will be how to fund it. How much will it cost to establish the archives? Will it involve renovating an existing space, building a new one, or renting space? Once it is established, what will the costs be to maintain it? Will the duties of the archives be contained within an existing position, or will a new position be proposed? Whether or not you can crunch the numbers yourself, it is important to get help to understand basic costs in order to make a realistic proposal and to back it up with hard figures.

There are plenty of cost-saving methods available to create an archives. Many successful programs exist in converted spaces; some are located within historic buildings. Shelving and furniture can often be purchased through government contracts. Consider seeking supplemental funding from grant sources, including local foundations, state library re-granting programs, and federal agencies, such as the National Historical Publications and Records Commission (NHPRC). For example, NHPRC funded the start-up costs for the San Antonio Municipal Archives, housed in a converted warehouse. The program, administered under the city clerk of the City of San Antonio, provided the funding for an archivist position as an in-kind match for the federal grant. Anywhere you can identify cost savings in the planning process will help make your case.

One issue that must be addressed is the matter of preserving electronic records. Electronic documents with permanent value are no different than their paper counterparts. While they do not take up physical space, they are just as problematic as paper. Be sure to factor in the costs of storage—whether it is maintained within the department, in conjunction with an information technology department, or through a third-party vendor. Cost analyses can help determine which way to go. Also, who will maintain the records? Will certain duties become a part of existing positions, or will a new position be created to specifically handle electronic records?

One often overlooked but very important concern is the audience. Who are or will be your users? Is it the government staff member who needs access to old minutes or audit reports, the historian or genealogist using court records, the journalist who desires photographs and documents relating to government hot topics, the taxpayer with questions about deeds, or the lawyer inquiring into zoning decisions from twenty-five years ago? Which system will work best for the majority of users and still be feasible for the government? Do you send archival records to the state archives when the capitol is a six-hour drive away? Is a centralized records center and archives a better option than joining with a local cooperative archives program? The key point is that any of these options are valid if determined to be economical and workable.

Lastly, support and buy-in for an archives program from top management is vital to success. Whether your leaders are a city council, county commissioners, a board of aldermen, or the board of directors of a historical society, it is important to capture their interest and advocate for your program to ensure continued funding and organizational stability. Perhaps the simplest method of generating interest is to provide them reproductions of historic images. The history buffs in the group are usually the first to see value and are not a hard sell. Offering tours for officials and their constituents is another easy way to familiarize them with your operation.

While it's great to tout the significance of historical photographs and visually arresting items in the collection, it's also important to demonstrate the archives' value in protecting government assets. By using documents, photographs, and maps of such things as parks and government-owned buildings and facilities as examples, you can show how archives support the restoration of historic structures, uncover the hidden history of a piece of land, or prevent adverse legal actions against the government. Once it is clear that the archives serves a diverse mix of both internal and external customers, it is easier to justify your existence.

Be sure to tout the legal and operational business benefits of an archives as well. Faster access to information means a faster resolution of a potential problem. In one example, a municipality was sued by the heirs of a family that donated a sizeable park used as a golf course. The heirs claimed the donors didn't approve of the use of the land for the golf course. The archives then produced correspondence with the donors endorsing the development of the golf course. The lawsuit was dismissed, and the city avoided losing many millions of dollars in lost property and golfing revenue.

An archives also provides transparency in government, an issue that is frequently raised by citizens. Accountability and integrity of information is an important foundation of a good local government. By researching state, federal, and local laws regarding archives and records, you can also make the statement that an archives and records program is a form of compliance with records laws, especially in the case of preserving and protecting documents. If a government's historical records are at risk of destruction through improper storage or are inaccessible, there may be a danger of violating legal mandates for the preservation of certain classes of records.

Mandates can be expressed within municipal or county ordinances in a number of ways. In the city of Seattle's archives and records management ordinance, one section outlines the responsibilities of elected officials and agency directors and managers, charging them to "adopt and implement policies regarding the creation and preservation of records," and to "establish safeguards against unauthorized or unlawful removal, loss or destruction of City records." The Seattle ordinance furthermore states that "Records of the City of Seattle shall be managed according to the controlling provisions of the Revised Code of Washington, Washington Administrative Code and this Chapter."[5]

It's also a good idea to couch your discussion of the value of archives in terms of assets versus liabilities. If your local government contains a risk management program, that office can be an important ally in convincing management that the proper care of permanent records is a safeguard against any number of threats—whether natural (flood, earthquake, tornado) or manmade (neglect, fire, vandalism, theft, terrorism). Risk assessments and reports can be very convincing tools when making a pitch and can explain the value of archives in very black and white terms.

Planning for an archives program early in its existence can prevent a number of problems. However, existing programs can also benefit greatly from enhancements that strengthen its ability to conduct business efficiently and independent of political manipulation. In short, an archives and records program is not just a good thing, it is also a good business practice.

## NOTES

1. Seattle Ordinance Number 124217 (creating a Seattle Archives and Records Management Program; amending Seattle Municipal Code (SMC) Chapter 3.122; repealing SMC Chapter 3.123; amending SMC Chapter 3.42.040; repealing SMC Chapter 3.42.050; and amending SMC Chapter 3.125), City of Seattle Municipal Code.

2. "Chapter 39c—Records Management Program," *Dallas City Code of Civil and Criminal Ordinances*, accessed July 14, 2014, http://www.amlegal.com/nxt/gateway.dll/Texas/dallas/volumei/preface?f=templates$fn=default.htm$3.0$vid=amlegal:dallas_tx.

3. Records Management, Archival and Storage, § 8.500—8.502, "Chapter 8—County Assets," Multnomah County Code, revised October 2, 2014.

4. "Rutherford County Archives," accessed July 2014, http://www.rutherfordcountytn.gov/archives/index.htm.

5. Seattle Ordinance Number 124217.

# 5

## Physical Considerations

Local government archives have most of the physical concerns that are present in other types of archives. Meeting the twin goals of preservation and access is a vitally important achievement in any archives and should be thought of as a sort of balancing act. Without preservation, archival records are doomed to a short lifespan through such damaging actions as mishandling and neglect. Without access, what good is it to preserve materials that only sit on a shelf unused? Efforts have to be made to improve access while minimizing damage to historical records.

### HOLDINGS MAINTENANCE

Preserving historical records for current and future use is a basic cornerstone of activity in any archives. Holdings maintenance is the act of stabilizing materials by doing things that will help extend the life of paper records and slow down the aging process. Most of this is achieved through improving the physical storage environment by using appropriate folders, boxes, and shelving and by keeping temperature and humidity levels within proper ranges. Holdings maintenance includes a wide variety of activities that are put into use daily by archivists. Using acid-free folders and boxes and photocopying newspaper clippings onto cotton-rag paper properly sized for the documents is done as collections are processed.

Preserving records includes caring for photographs, audio, and moving images and may mean copying and reformatting records. Taking care to regulate temperature and humidity levels and using proper lighting are ongoing tasks done in cooperation with building maintenance or equipment contractors.

Having proper security and fire alarms and developing disaster plans so that your archives and staff are ready in case of flood, fire, or storms are all important parts of holdings maintenance. Readers desiring more information on the topics and subjects discussed here are encouraged to learn more through websites and books described in the bibliography located at the end of the book.

### Preservation versus Conservation

It is important here to make a distinction between two terms frequently confused: preservation and conservation. *Preservation* is actions that help extend the life of documents. It involves preventive measures to slow down the inevitable disintegration of paper and other materials, such as providing stable housing in the form of archival folders and boxes, removing damaging fasteners (staples and paperclips), flattening and unrolling, and controlling the storage environment (through adjusting lighting, temperature, and relative humidity). Preservation is different from conservation because it does not involve altering the document. Many types of preservation are in effect stop-gap measures to prevent further problems or slow down an existing problem.

*Conservation* is the process of reversing damage to documents through specific treatments. Repairing and mending tears in documents, removing damaging adhesives such as tape and glue, and cleaning dirt and soot from documents are all forms of conservation. Conservation treatments should be performed only by a trained conservator. While archivists can learn to do simple paper mending, it is often better left to professionals with expertise in conservation methods. You will find many examples in an archives of documents that a well-meaning amateur has tried to mend or repair, usually with disastrous results. For example, the use of adhesive tapes (most notoriously "Scotch tape") should be avoided at all costs. Similarly, do not use resin craft glue, or school glue, which is sometimes used to repair bound items and to hold spines together.

## HOUSING

Housing is perhaps the most important part of the preservation process. Without reliable protective housing, archival materials are at risk of damage and destruction due to careless or inappropriate handling. Local government archives utilize all of the types of housing found in most other repositories, including Hollinger boxes (a flip-top box, dimensions approximately 15 x 5 x 10 inches); cubic foot boxes (approximately 15 x 12 x 10 inches); and other boxes that can be ordered in a wide range of sizes and shapes.

The need for stable housing for archival documents is due to the variance in quality of the paper used in government offices. Paper made before the advent of bleaching and alum and rosin sizing in the mid-to-late-nineteenth century often has a higher cotton fiber content and is generally more stable than paper made later. In government archives, this paper is often found in ledger books. Most paper made during the last one hundred twenty-five years was and is mass-produced by methods that created inexpensive and bright paper. The paper, however, is prone to chemical decomposition, breaking down the paper fibers and making the paper more and more brittle. While decay is nearly impossible to stop, it can be slowed down significantly when maintained in non-acidic folders and containers.

## Archival Boxes

Boxes and folders said to be "archival" are made of acid-free cardboard and paper, meaning the board or paper is manufactured to have a pH value of 6.0 or higher. Acid-free products provide a stable environment for acidic paper dating from the late nineteenth century to the present—the paper which is typically found in government offices. Boxes and folders perform the two most vital functions of preservation—keeping paper flat and rigidly supported, and keeping damaging light away from the paper.

Boxes traditionally used in archives come in a number of standard sizes. The *Hollinger box* is a flip-top document box that was developed for use by the federal government in the 1940s by William K. Hollinger, hence the name. It is widely used and made by a number of different archives suppliers. The next most common box used in archives is the *cubic foot box*, sometimes called a "banker's box" or a records center carton. If you are purchasing cubic foot boxes, it is wise to select double-walled construction boxes instead of single, which collapse easily when stacked. The greatest advantage of using Hollinger boxes and cubic foot boxes is that they are a standardized size. Standardized sizes mean that shelving can be configured to hold the most boxes economically without wasting valuable space.

Materials that are too large for these boxes and must be stored flat can be housed in oversized boxes that are sometimes called a print box. Maps, plans, posters, prints, and drawings on larger paper can be housed in flat files, sometimes called map cabinets. When planning a storage area for archival materials, be sure to set aside room for flat files and shelving configured for oversized boxes.

It is important to ensure that records fit in the most suitable size of container. Materials crammed into a box that is too small run the risk of being warped or damaged; materials stored in a box that is too large are in danger of shifting inside the box and being damaged whenever the box is moved.

**Figure 5.1.** Document boxes, sometimes called Hollinger boxes, are an efficient way to house letter- and legal-sized paper. Standardized box sizes economize storage space. Photo by John H. Slate, Dallas Municipal Archives, City of Dallas, TX.

## Folders

Folders, like boxes, are among the first line of defense against light damage and dust and provide a rigid support for paper that can easily curl or become creased or tear. Use folders that are manufactured with acid-free cardstock, just as you do with boxes. Many suppliers offer a wide range of folder sizes, the most common being letter and legal sizes, but also with variations on these sizes and with varying folder tab cuts (e.g., full-cut, half-cut, and several cut dimensions in between). Map folders and other large oversized folders are sold in standardized sizes and made from acid-free cardstock, and can be cut down and customized for use.

## Housing for Oversized Records

Archivists typically measure volume in linear feet and sometimes cubic feet when stored on shelves. Measuring your archives' holdings is essential for space planning, as well as to set goals for archival processing. As defined in the Society of American Archivists' *Glossary of Archival and Records*

*Terminology*, "A linear foot measures twelve inches for documents stored on edge, or twelve inches high for documents stored horizontally. For letter size documents, it is slightly less than a cubic foot."[1] Cubic foot measurement is the three-dimensional measurement of a foot expressed as twelve inches wide by twelve inches high by twelve inches deep. Note that the actual volume capacity for a box should be measured by the *interior* dimensions, which are slightly smaller than the exterior dimensions.

## Oversized Records

Nearly all local government archives contain ledgers or bound books of some kind, widely varying in size and composition. Other oversized documents found in local government archives include maps, plans, and architectural drawings. Because they can be unwieldy, oversized items require special care and handling to prevent damage. When transporting folders to and from storage areas to research areas, take care not to bend or crease folders. In the research area, be sure to have a large enough table to lay out oversized items or risk damage through poor support.

Figure 5.2. Tax ledgers from the late 19th century are often found in local government archives. Ledgers and other oversized formats present storage as well as preservation challenges. Photo by John H. Slate, Dallas Municipal Archives, City of Dallas, TX.

*Ledgers* were a preferred method of recording information in governments for centuries but are less popular today because it is easier to handle and store standardized paper sizes such as 8.5 × 11 inches (letter) and 8.5 × 14 inches (legal). Ledgers usually have either sewn bindings, like a book, or post bindings or loose-leaf bindings, which both allow for pages to be added or removed without damage. The boards or outer covers of ledgers for many years were made of a combination of cloth, paper, and leather. Because decorative leather bindings are made through a chemical tanning process, the leather eventually disintegrates chemically and leaves a fine powder commonly called "red rot." This powder stains the hands and is difficult to wash out of clothing. Be sure to use gloves to handle volumes that have red rot, and wash hands after use.[2]

*Architectural and engineering plans* of local government facilities, structures, and infrastructure (such as bridges, roads, and water and sewer lines) are very common to local government archives. They can be made of everything from starched cotton fabric to tracing paper to blueprint paper to polyester film. Oversized plans and drawings are best stored flat, unless their size is compromised by an inadequate folder. If the plans won't fit comfortably into a folder or into a flat file cabinet, consider interleaving the sheets with acid-free tissue and rolling for long-term storage.

Sometimes oversized plans and drawings arrive in the archives folded, flattened, or rolled. It is preferable to flatten them and store them flat as long as they fit in a folder. Flattening folded and rolled items requires care and patience and is described in detail in the book *Architectural Records: Managing Design and Construction Records.*[3] Never force a tightly rolled item open; paper and other media may be brittle and can tear easily.

*Scrapbooks and photo albums* are traditionally associated with individuals or groups, but are sometimes found in local government archives. Most often they document a specific department or a specific event or project. While older scrapbooks and albums may be composed of brittle and acidic paper, resist the temptation to remove items from the pages or disassemble the bindings. Disrupting the sequence of the items destroys context (the order, or storyline of the images or items), and also puts individual pieces at risk of damage or mutilation. To prevent pages from sticking together or harming the items on the facing page, interleave pages with acid-free tissue or paper.

*Bound items*, regardless of size, should be handled carefully with respect to the bindings. Improper storage and use can weaken bindings and loosen the outer boards. To prevent further stress on the bindings, you can either purchase or make supports to place under the open bound volume, called a cradle.

Figure 5.3.    Flat oversized documents such as architectural and engineering plans can be maintained flat in special file cabinets. Image courtesy Multnomah County (OR) Archives.

Figure 5.4. Oversized documents too large for map cabinets can be safely stored rolled and protected from dust and light damage. Image courtesy Multnomah County (OR) Archives.

## Photography

Few people need convincing that photography is one of the most important types of document that can be found in a local government archives. Photography provides evidence of governmental activities, elected officials and staff, their work spaces and surroundings, buildings and structures built or owned by the government, documentation of departmental business and projects, and events and occasions involving the government. Photography is a record of how business was done, as well as a record of how government interacts with citizens.

There have been many different formats and types of photography since its introduction in the late 1830s, though by and large most local government archives have twentieth-century formats such as gelatin silver prints and negatives in their collections. A few local governments may have late nineteenth-century formats such as albumen prints and glass-plate negatives. The sources for photography in local governments are equally varied, from in-house agencies such as a public information office or an official county

Figure 5.5a.   Book supports, wedges or a cradle (shown here) preserve bound items so
the volume can be opened comfortably without stressing the bindings. Courtesy City of
Portland Archives & Records Center.

or city photographer, to photography made by individual government departments. In a few cases, nongovernment records such as photography belonging to individuals may find their way into a local government collection.

Some departments—such as a water department or a public works department—create large volumes of photos to document engineering projects. Photographs of flood protection and levee building may hold more interest for internal users, but images of floods and natural disasters are perennial favorites for newspapers, television stations, and social media. Photographs of historic structures in a community are especially valued for their details of construction and provide a wealth of information and clues for preservation and conservation.

A full-scale discussion here of the care and handling of photography in archives is limited by space, but there are some basic things that every person working with archival materials should know and practice. Always handle photographic prints and negatives by their edges, taking care not to place damaging oily fingerprints on the surface of film or prints. It is always a good idea to wear cotton gloves to handle photography. Be sure to issue gloves to

**Figure 5.5b.** Hurricanes often impact local government records. Here water-soaked records from the Orleans Parish Criminal Court are being removed from the Clerk of Courts office. Photo by Karl Niederer. Courtesy of Council of State Archivists.

researchers using photographic materials, and keep several clean pairs ready for use by yourself, researchers, and colleagues. Never mark the back of a photo print with ink; only use soft lead pencil. Even when using pencil, don't press too hard on thinner prints or you'll risk embossing the image on the front. If you add information to the back of photos, such as accession numbers, write only on the outer edges with your pencil.

Sleeving prints and negatives (discussed in the next section) is the best defense against abrasion, contact with skin, and light damage. Photographic prints are often sleeved with polyester (Mylar or Melinex), and negatives are frequently stored in sleeves made of polypropylene or polyethylene with narrow seams configured for 35- and 120-millimeter strips. To prevent bowing and bending, prints and negatives are best stored flat in horizontal print boxes, but can be stored upright in document boxes if there is enough material to keep the prints flat and rigid.

Before the advent of plastics, negatives were made on glass. Should you find glass plate negatives among government records, they should be handled carefully to avoid breakage. Pack them carefully in boxes identified with "fragile" signage on the outside so it is easily seen. Most plastic-based film made since the 1940s is easily identified on the edges with the wording "safety film," and can be stored safely. However, be aware of nitrate-based photographic film, which is chemically unstable and at risk of disintegration. The decomposing chemicals in nitrate film make it very combustible and a genuine fire hazard. Sheet film is less of a risk than roll film or motion picture film, which may be found stored in canisters, but nonetheless should be segregated from other kinds of film.

"Born-digital" photography is discussed in depth in chapter 7, "Electronic Records." For a book-length discussion on photography in archives, please consult *Photographs: Archival Care and Management*, by Mary Lynn Ritzenthaler and Diane Vogt-O'Connor, published by the Society of American Archivists.

## Audio and Moving-Image Materials

Many archives have sizeable volumes of non-paper records, including audio and moving-image recordings. *Audio* can be found in many different formats in archives, both modern and historic. For instance, the Dallas Municipal Archives contains audio in audio cassettes, seven-inch reel-to-reel tapes, digital audio files, and even sixteen-inch transcription phonograph discs. Other archives have extensive collections of videos from government-operated television stations.

Audio in a local government is most commonly found in the form of meeting recordings, usually of the governing body, but it can also include meetings of boards and commissions reporting to the governing body or as evidence from interviews in law enforcement files. In most states, written minutes of meetings and written arrest reports are considered the official record of a meeting and thus the recording is more often than not kept for convenience. Other recordings may include speeches or audio of events involving elected officials or public hearings. Bear in mind that not every recording must be saved. The appraisal process (see chapter 6 for a discussion of appraisal) can help decide what is most valuable to the archives and what is less valuable and does not need to be retained permanently.

The largest obstacle to accessing audio is technology. If you don't have a reel-to-reel tape deck or a cassette deck, you can find used ones for sale online or through local resale markets. Even if you are able to play back audio, you're still be stuck with an obsolete format. Mass digitization transfer services are available, but involve a cost. It is entirely possible to configure your own digital transfer station inexpensively, but you will want to weigh its cost effectiveness against the labor and time involved.

Take great care in using playback equipment, especially for magnetic tape. Improperly stored, tape can dry out and the coating on the polyester tape base can flake off. Consult an audiotape professional in this case and don't attempt your own transfer. Similarly, the tape in both open reels and inside winding mechanisms in cassettes can easily get tangled and creased. When in doubt, don't subject the tape to further possible abuse.

*Moving-image materials* refers to motion picture film and videotape. There are two kinds of moving-image materials normally found in local governments—programs made in-house by a government department, such as a police or fire department—and programs that are commercially made, such as training films and videos. Concentrate on the items made inside government, as they are a unique and true government record; commercially made training movies are usually not rare and are likely to be found in local governments throughout the country.

It isn't always possible, but transferring film and videotape to a digital form is the best way to create a viewing copy that both protects the original from damage and makes it accessible for viewing. Grants are available at the federal level and frequently at the local level for converting film.

## BASIC PRESERVATION TREATMENTS

Besides rehousing materials, several further options for preservation will help your archives survive into the future.

In spite of an archivist's well-meaning intention of keeping items together, many documents suffer damage through the use of *different kinds of fasteners*.

Typical fasteners in a government office setting include paperclips, staples, grommets, brads, and other sorts of binding tools. In a humid environment, paperclips and staples can rust and leave rusty residue on paper, which in time can actually eat through the paper. Most paperclips can be removed carefully by hand or with the assistance of a hand tool. Staples can be removed with traditional staple removers, but care should be exercised to prevent tearing and gouging the paper. Because grommets and other fasteners are sometimes configured unusually, do not attempt to pry them loose if the paper looks like it will tear. With any fasteners, if there is any indication you might damage the paper, it is best to simply leave it alone.

Another preservation treatment is *sleeving: enclosing or encapsulating with plastics*. This does *not* include lamination, a long-discredited practice that will damage documents and should be completely avoided. Lamination involves fusing paper documents with thin layers of plastic and cannot be undone. Loose protective enclosures for encapsulating documents are acceptable and can include plastic sleeves and customized plastic sheets. Plastic sleeving offers a number of preservation benefits: it keeps dust and fingerprint oils away from the item's surface; reduces abrasion; and can block harmful ultraviolet light. Additionally, the added thickness of the plastic or polyester can provide extra support for items that are thin and flimsy by nature or, in the case of nineteenth-century photo prints mounted on cardboard, a degree of stability when the mount is cracked or weakened.

Commercially made plastic sleeves of polyester, polypropylene, or polyethylene are among the most common plastic enclosures and are manufactured in standardized sizes to match the most common sizes of documents, prints, and photographs. Polyester film can also be purchased by the roll and trimmed to create custom sleeves.

Professional archivists commonly use polyester film sold under the names Mylar or Melinex, which is suitable for archival materials because it is made of inert plastic, meaning it does not give off invisible gases that are harmful to paper and other items. Avoid at all costs using enclosures made of polyvinyl chloride, or PVC. When purchasing sleeving and housing supplies for photographic archival material, investigate whether the materials have passed the Photographic Activity Test, or PAT, an international standard test (ISO18916) for evaluating archival photographic storage products.[4]

## Degraded Paper and Preservation Photocopying

Local government archives contain many different kinds of paper. Some of it is made of inexpensive materials and inks which are not meant to be permanent. Newsprint, Thermofax, spirit masters (ditto), early Xerox, Photostats, telefacsimile, and thermal receipt paper present significant preservation challenges that must be addressed. The words and images on many of these kinds of papers fade quickly, and in some cases can disappear entirely. The volatile chemicals in these documents will damage adjacent paper if left next to other paper indefinitely. Photocopying onto acid-free paper is a standard preservation measure when any of these kinds of paper are encountered. Whether originals are kept or not after photocopying, be sure they are segregated from other materials to prevent any further damage.

Newspaper clippings in particular are well known as a hazard among archival materials. When left in a file facing other paper, the newspaper acidifies and leaves an acidic stain on the adjoining paper. Once photocopied, the original clipping can be discarded.[5] The photocopy is thus treated as the archival copy. On a larger scale, large runs of newspapers have traditionally been committed to microfilm. The film can be used many times without subjecting originals to further abuse. More recently, newspapers or the microfilm itself is scanned for online access. While the originals are generally retained, the scanned copies are much easier to use.

## Environmental Control

In addition to providing proper housing, controlling the environment of the archives is the most important thing you can do to improve the stability and longevity of archival materials. Controlling or mitigating temperature, humidity, and lighting and eliminating potential pests can be difficult or easy, depending on your building and your resources. Whether your archives program is well funded or not, there are plenty of improvements that can be implemented, ranging from low or no cost up to expensive ones.

*A clean environment* as free from dirt and dust as possible is just as important as controlling temperature or humidity. Dust accumulates faster in some storage areas than others, so keep archives areas swept at intervals that makes sense for your situation. Sweeping is not only good for picking up dirt, but it also provides an opportunity to examine for insects. Scheduling periodic sweeping and dusting of shelves will pay off in the long run and prevent excessive dust buildup. The musty smell common in some archives can be an indicator of poor air flow, as well as problems with dust buildup. Be sure your air-conditioning system has proper filtering and that the filters are changed out periodically. Ventilation with fans can also ensure that there is constant air circulation in the vault or storage area.

*Lighting* is another type of environmental control that can be achieved fairly simply. Archives storage areas should be as dark as possible to prevent light damage. If your storage area has its own light switch, be sure it can be turned off whenever the room is not in use. Lighting used in storage areas should be incandescent or LED (Light-Emitting-Diode) if possible. If you are stuck with traditional lighting such as fluorescent tube fixtures, consider purchasing clear protective sleeves that will filter the harmful ultraviolet light.

Controlling temperature and humidity levels can do much to extend the life of archival records, especially if you have good controls in your storage room. Does your storage facility share its *HVAC* (heating, ventilation, and air-conditioning) system with the rest of the building, or does it have its own unit? Ideally you want to have a stand-alone unit that will allow for keeping the temperature at recommended levels, which are usually too cold for work spaces. If your storage area is heated and cooled with the rest of the building, you may not have as much control over temperature and relative humidity. In that case, you should still commit to monitoring fluctuations in temperature through a hygrothermograph data logger.

Hygrothermograph data loggers are inexpensive devices that automatically collect temperature and Rh data on a twenty-four-hour basis and allow you to see how consistent the levels are. Unstable levels are undesirable and can shorten the life of paper-based materials. One of the primary benefits of using data loggers is the ability to automatically collect data for whatever duration of time you wish. The data can then be downloaded from the logger to review a comprehensive picture of the environmental conditions being monitored. You can use information you gather from data loggers to adjust temperatures and possibly to convince funders to upgrade HVAC equipment in the storage area.

If you don't have a budget for improving the environment in storage areas, there are several things you can do that are low cost or no cost. According to the Northeast Document Conservation Center, keeping your HVAC at one level twenty-four hours a day will help prevent major fluctuations in temperature and humidity. Particularly in governments, HVAC units are sometimes shut down at night or over weekends and holidays to save money. The long-term damage to collections due to significant fluctuations will outweigh the immediate cost-saving benefits. Weather stripping and sealing doors and windows are other low-cost measures. If you're in an area with long winters, keep excessive heating down during the season and the temperature preferably around 65° F. Don't overheat, which can increase humidity, as well as tempt employees to let in outside air and destabilize the environment.[6]

## SECURITY

Because local government archival records contain legal, historical, administrative, intrinsic, and other kinds of value, they must be kept safe and secure. Archival materials are tempting targets for thieves because they may have value on the black market and even on online auction and shopping sites such as e-Bay. Records from the seventeenth, eighteenth, and nineteenth centuries as well as items with the signatures of major political figures may be objects of desire for private collectors. Thieves can come in the form of both researchers and sadly even inside staff, so vigilance and precaution are paramount. Researchers have been known to cultivate relationships with staff members to the point where they are trusted more than they should be. A sheriff's deputy from a neighboring county, for example, managed to steal many documents from a county archives after the small staff allowed him to be alone with records.

Fortunately, government facilities are usually already outfitted with some security features, such as controlled access points into the building, patrolling security staff and monitored hallways, and camera systems to detect unauthorized entry or activity. Be sure that research areas, staff-only areas, and storage areas are distinct and separated by locked doors (or doors that can be locked) to make clear where researchers can and cannot travel. The use of lockers for personal belongings should be an important feature of your research area and sends a strong message that users are under supervision at all times.

Only designated facilities staff and archives staff should have access to storage areas; limit the number of sets of keys or electronic keypad passwords distributed to reduce the chances of unauthorized entry. Doors to storage areas should remain locked when not in use, and clerical staff and volunteers should use a set of keys that are kept in a central location for use only during opening hours. Don't allow keys to leave the premises if at all possible. Some archives include a secondary gated anteroom to further discourage theft. When closing for the day, always test doors and locked gating to ensure locks are engaged. If your facility uses a keypad alarm system, be sure you know how to arm and disarm it quickly, and have security force contacts available should there be an accidental alarm failure.

## PEST CONTROL

Pest control should involve not just the elimination of insects and vermin, but also their mitigation and prevention. Instead of following the typical reactive approach to finding and killing pests, consider integrated pest management, which focuses on long-term prevention through biological control, monitoring, and modification of human practices around the archives. Rather than using poisons and messy chemicals for insects, consider using glue traps, boric acid, and diatomaceous earth, which are safer for the environment and easier to clean up. Glue traps and regular walk-throughs are very visible ways to see what kinds of pests are entering, as well as the volume. Similarly for rats and mice, traps are more sound ecologically and can be used repeatedly. The best way to manage rodents is through good sanitation inside and outside, and rat-proofing inside by sealing cracks and openings and plugging holes with substances rats won't chew through, like steel wool.

Even if you can't control your entire building, archives areas under your control should be kept free of food trash and garbage should be emptied daily. Remind staff to remove food trash and eat only in designated areas. If you hold receptions or other events that include food, be sure it is removed the same day. It is helpful to keep staff break rooms, or places with refrigerators and microwave ovens fully apart from storage and research areas.

When receiving new collections from outside your building, take the time to examine boxes outside for any visual signs of insect infestation. Silverfish and cockroaches especially can easily hide within the folds of paper and survive the journey into a new environment. Infested collections can be treated with flash-freezing, which can be contracted from businesses with large freezers, or from a disaster recovery business that has freezing chambers specifically designed to accommodate paper-based records and boxes. Fumigation can also be done but is generally performed on large-scale infestations.

## NEW AND RENOVATED BUILDINGS

Too often archives are assigned the least desirable space in a building. In courthouses and other local government buildings, storage areas are shoe-horned into basements, boiler rooms, attics, former office spaces, and even jail cells. What they all have in common is that each space was not originally configured or constructed to house archival materials. Frequently we have little or no choice in the space we are assigned, so it's important to learn how to adapt and work around obstacles.

The optimum storage area is one without windows or a way for outside light to penetrate. Storage spaces for archival materials first and foremost should be away from windows whenever possible. If you are limited in space choices and forced to utilize a room with windows, consider a window treatment that will block ultraviolet light and reflect heat away. Light-blocking films and foils can be found that do not detract from a building's outside appearance.

**Figure 5.6a.** The Troup County Archives in LaGrange, Georgia, is one of many archives housed in renovated historic buildings—in this case, a 100-year old bank building. Photo by Kaye Lanning Minchew.

Shelving can come in many different configurations and is manufactured from a number of materials, most frequently steel. Powder-coated steel is preferable to sprayed enamel paint due to the gases emitted from sprayed enamel that are harmful to paper (commonly called "off-gassing"). If you are using existing shelving, examine for signs of rust and discontinue use of any parts that are rusty. Standardized shelving can be purchased in units to create ranges and can be customized for width and depth, especially useful if you have oversized materials that won't fit in flat file drawers. Do not use wooden shelving for storage, no matter how handsome the cabinet or ranges look. Most wooden furniture is finished with varnishes that off-gas and will harm paper.

The spacing of shelving is often dictated by the size of the space and such required allowances as door clearance. A common aisle width is thirty-six inches to allow for comfortable movement of book trucks and dollies, but you will also want to give consideration to requirements specified in the Americans with Disabilities Act and recommendations of such groups as the Occupational Safety & Health Administration (OSHA).

**Figure 5.6b.** Tattnall County Archives in Reidsville, Georgia, uses an old jail for its records storage. Two of the original cells remain so boxes are stored on the bed platforms. Photo by Kaye Lanning Minchew, used with permission of Tattnall County Archives committee.

## Fire and Flooding Safety

Fire safety should never be overlooked. There cannot be enough emphasis placed upon the importance of making sure there is some kind of fire suppression system in place. Fire detection equipment, usually meaning smoke detectors and smoke alarms, are an important defense and should be checked regularly for proper operation. Learn what kinds of fire suppression equipment are in your building and specifically in the archives. Sprinkler systems are the most common and are automatically activated by heat and/or smoke. Although it would seem sprinklers are not suitable for protecting paper-based records, remember the records are in boxes and on metal shelves which can shield the contents for a short time.

Figure 5.7.   The archives of Baldwin County, Alabama, located in Bay Minette, is in a building built specifically to house the county's permanently valuable records. Photo courtesy of Baldwin County Archives, AL.

Some buildings have standpipes, which deliver water to connected fire hoses. Hoses are sometimes curled into boxes mounted to walls. Because hoses are unwieldy and hard to handle, employees are usually discouraged from trying to use them. Handheld fire extinguishers are very common and it's a good idea to have a building plan marking their locations. Although it is much more likely employees will be evacuated from a building to make way for firefighters, it is still worthwhile to learn how to operate a handheld extinguisher. Fire marshals and fire prevention units in local fire departments sometimes offer demonstrations for staff upon request. Conduct an annual inspection to ensure fire extinguishers are operational and ready for use.

Plan ahead for disasters and how to get out of your facility safely. Doors and emergency exits should be clearly marked in both storage areas and reference areas, and maps or plans showing exit routes should be distributed to all employees and volunteers. Having a written and annually updated disaster plan is vital to caring for archives materials after or if you are allowed back inside the building. The Council of State Archivists (COSA) hosts a wealth of information on its website regarding emergency preparedness and recovery, specifically written for state and local governments. It includes disaster recovery methods, how to find and select vendors for disaster recovery services, and information-specific topics such as tornadoes and mold remediation: http://www.statearchivists.org/arc/states/res_disa.htm.

Figure 5.8.  Fires have ruined many government records over the centuries. The Hancock County, Georgia, archives fire of August 14, 2014, destroyed the 1883 courthouse and practically all of the county's historic records, some dating to the 1790s. Many of the archives' documents, however, were previously microfilmed. Photo courtesy of Anne S. Floyd, CSRA Regional Commission.

Because so many archives are located within building basements, the danger of flooding is a very real challenge that should be monitored if there is any reason to believe flooding is possible. The first and most frequent cause is plumbing failure. Another common problem is flooding from heavy rain, which can create runoff and excess moisture, sometimes penetrating the building's envelope if the waterproofing seal around the building fails. Moisture detectors are inexpensive and can be fitted into a floor where archives materials are stored, setting off an alarm if the presence of water or moisture is discerned.

If you are fortunate to oversee or provide input into the construction of a dedicated archives space, you will want to become familiar with standards and best practices for archives construction. Thomas P. Wilsted's book *Planning New and Remodeled Archival Facilities* (Society of American Archivists, 2007), is a valuable guide to the decision-making process regarding what kind of building to erect, and the many issues to consider before the construction begins.

Figure 5.9.   Fires have ruined many government records over the centuries. The Hancock County, Georgia, archives fire of August 14, 2014, destroyed the 1883 courthouse and practically all of the county's historic records, some dating to the 1790s. Many of the archives' documents, however, were previously microfilmed. Photo courtesy of Anne S. Floyd, CSRA Regional Commission.

Two sets of guidelines and best practices for the construction of archives facilities are Diane Vogt O'Connor's *Archival and Special Collections Facilities* and the National Archives' *Memorandum NARA 1571, Archival Storage Standards.*[7] Each of these writings prescribe some goals and objectives that are difficult or impossible to achieve under modest budgets, but it is nonetheless worthwhile to understand what is considered optimal and that some ideals and best practices can be incorporated into your plan through less complicated and inexpensive means. Text may frequently refer to published standards, which are issued by the International Standards Organization (ISO) or the American National Standards Institute (ANSI). Archivists need to do all they can to preserve materials. Often that gets accomplished by doing a little at a time and being ready if funds become available for improvements to the building and the heating and air-conditioning system.

## NOTES

1. Richard Pearce-Moses, *A Glossary of Archival and Records Terminology* (Chicago: Society of American Archivists, 2005), 234.

2. Marion Kite and Roy Thomson, eds., *Conservation of Leather and Related Materials* (New York: Routledge), 60–62.

3. Waverly Lowell and Tawny Ryan Nelb, *Architectural Records: Managing Design and Construction Records* (Chicago: Society of American Archivists, 2006), 110–11.

4. Mary Lynn Ritzenthaler and Diane Vogt O'Connor, *Photographs: Archival Care and Management* (Chicago: Society of American Archivists, 2006), 225–26.

5. Norvell M. M. Jones, "Archival Copies of Thermofax, Verifax, and Other Unstable Records," National Archives Technical Information paper No. 5 (1990); Association for Library Collections and Technical Services, "Guidelines for Preservation Photocopying of Replacement Pages" (1990), accessed September 22, 2015, http://www.ala.org/alcts/resources/preserv/presvphotocop.

6. Northeast Document Conservation Center, *Low Cost/No Cost Improvements in Climate Control*, accessed October 13, 2015, https://www.nedcc.org/free-resources/preservation-leaflets/2.-the-environment/2.6-low-costno-cost-improvements-in-climate-control.

7. Diane Vogt O'Connor, *Archival and Special Collections Facilities: Guidelines for Archivists, Librarians, Architects, and Engineers* (The Hague, Netherlands: International Federation of Library Associations and Institutions, 2012); National Archives and Records Administration, *Memorandum NARA 1571, Archival Storage Standards* (Washington, DC: The National Archives, 2001).

# 6

## Intellectual Considerations

**P**reparing archival materials for use by researchers and staff involves much more than physical actions. Preservation alone does not make archival materials accessible. From the point that a new collection enters the archives to the moment it is ready for researchers, there is a process that helps make it understandable and useful. *Appraisal*, sometimes called selection, determines which items have enduring or permanent value and thus makes them eligible for becoming a part of an archives. *Arrangement* and *description* ensures that a collection is organized and structured and that users can discover what the collection is about. The series of actions that make collections available for use is called *processing*.

Local government archives have a responsibility to its creators to provide materials to help government employees carry out their daily work. However, it is equally important that an archives be responsive to the community that funds and supports it.

### APPRAISING AND SELECTING LOCAL GOVERNMENT RECORDS

To keep or not to keep, that is one of the first questions to ask. The decision to accept a body of records can have a major impact upon an archives well into the future. How much space will it require for storage? While appraisal is sometimes viewed as an intellectual exercise, it is in many ways a very practical and essential function of archives management. While it is tempting to keep anything that looks interesting, archivists and records professionals must ask hard questions to justify the time, space, and expense of maintaining the materials.

If you are in a very old local government and you discover documents from the eighteenth century, it won't be hard to decide whether you should keep them. The rarity of any document from the 1700s alone, almost regardless of the subject matter, is enough to merit permanent care. Conversely, in much younger governments you are very likely to encounter mostly twentieth-century records, of which there is often much duplication. With the rise of inexpensive paper and reproduction methods comes the challenge of identifying what has truly permanent value, and what does not.

Evaluating the importance of records is at the core of archival appraisal. Archival theorist T. R. Schellenberg, in working with federal records, developed the notion that archives have two main values—primary and secondary. Primary value is the reason for which the documents were originally created, while secondary value is the usefulness of a document beyond its original function. Over time Schellenberg's ideas, and those of his predecessors, have been elaborated, refined further, and challenged by later theorists.[1]

Though there is much debate over definitions, several generally accepted types of value have been identified as criteria for selection. The *operational value* of records is its value to a government for conducting business. In the case of local governments, essential documents such as charters and civil and criminal codes have operational value because they include the statutory authority to act as a unit of local government and as an agency of a state and administer such services as public safety, public health, and transportation regulation.

The *fiscal value* of a body of records is its value in governmental financial transactions. Examples include land and property records, which may show how much a piece of property was purchased for and the price it later sells at, and audit reports, which examine the efficiency of business operations, frequently involving the flow of revenue.

The *historical value* of records is their usefulness to the study of and writing about the past. This type of value is exceptionally broad because it is subjective and can encompass almost any sort of record. Historical value might be applied to materials that are presumed to be beneficial in writing a history of a city or county.

The *intrinsic value* of a record is its worth as an object rather than its informational content. An example of a local government record having intrinsic value might be a document that is signed by an important elected official. The value is in its connection to a historic figure or event, rather than what can be learned from the document.

The *legal value* of records is their worth in both making laws and in the protection of public assets. For example, a record has legal value if it can be used to solve a property or boundary dispute in a local government. In another example, the keeping of superseded civil and criminal codes assist a government's legal department in the study and drafting of new laws.

The *monetary value* of records is like intrinsic value, in that a document has merit for itself and what it might bring if sold to a collector. A historic map, a court case from Colonial America, or an order signed by a young attorney named Abraham Lincoln are examples of items having monetary value.

Beyond the various types of value that have been described, there are other criteria that should be considered. For instance, are the records comprehensive, covering a sizeable span of time, or do they only reflect a short period of time? Uniqueness is another criterion. Is the information found only in this body of records, or can it be found elsewhere? Duplication is a sound reason to reject records.

Is there enough space necessary to house the collection? Many archives have had to decline collections due to space restrictions. Does the collection contain sensitive or restricted information that might create either a security issue, or freedom of information issues? Some local government archives have a ground rule of not accepting any materials that could be closed to the public for many years. Locally filed birth certificates that are closed to the public for seventy-five years or more may fall under this category, so it is a case-by-case decision to make this sort of material a part of an archives.

Not only do you need to have policies in place that describe what you will accept, but it is very important to have a mirror policy that states the kinds of things the archives *will not* accept. In local governments, there is a very clear and legal distinction between what is considered a government record and what is not. Plaques and ceremonial gifts presented to elected officials are examples of non-records that are sometimes offered to an archives. Three-dimensional artifacts are also not generally considered a record. While it would be tantalizing to be offered fire or police department uniforms from a century ago, an archives must decide whether it is in the business of preserving paper-based and electronic records strictly, or if it can also take on museum-related functions. If your community has a local history museum, it may be better equipped to both store and display things like clothing, firearms, and antique equipment. In other cases, the local government archives also serves as the local history museum. Much depends on the availability of space and funds and the mission of the archives.

Would your archives consider collecting the papers of elected officials? It truly boils down to which records are considered official papers, and which ones are considered private. It can be argued that the official records of elected officials are the meeting minutes, ordinances, resolutions, and decisions made by governing bodies, created in the course of their routine business. Greeting cards, private correspondence (as opposed to constituent correspondence), and papers not relating to government business are usually not considered government records.

While it might be enticing to preserve the records of a local official, will private correspondence, ceremonial plaques, private financial or medical

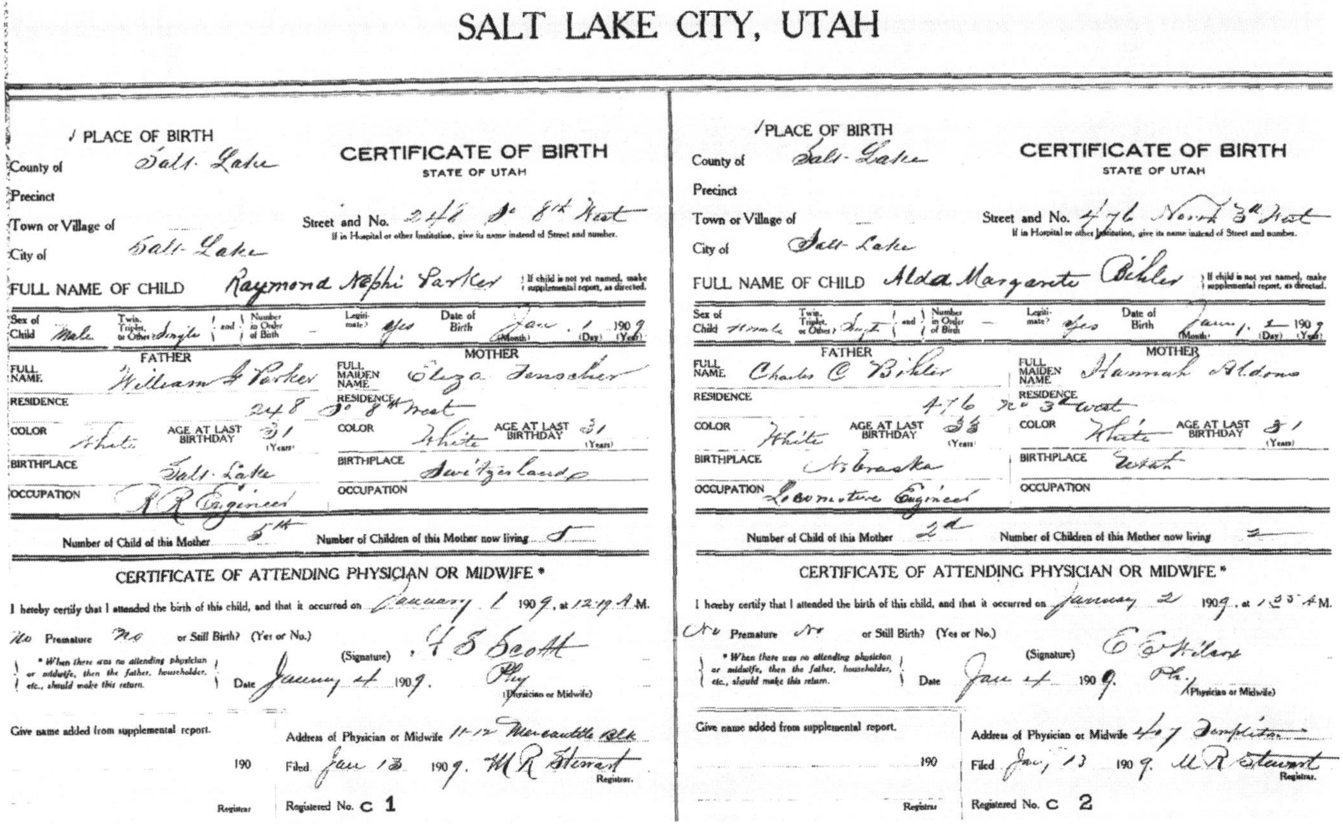

SALT LAKE CITY, UTAH

PLACE OF BIRTH
County of Salt Lake
Precinct
Town or Village of
City of Salt Lake

**CERTIFICATE OF BIRTH**
STATE OF UTAH

Street and No. 248 So 8th West
If in Hospital or other Institution, give its name instead of Street and number.

FULL NAME OF CHILD Raymond Nephi Parker (If child is not yet named, make supplemental report, as directed.)

Sex of Child Male | Twin, Triplet, or Other Single | and | Number in Order of Birth — | Legitimate? yes | Date of Birth Jan. 1 1909 (Month) (Day) (Year)

| FATHER | | MOTHER | |
|---|---|---|---|
| FULL NAME | William J Parker | FULL MAIDEN NAME | Eliza Janscher |
| RESIDENCE | 248 So 8th West | RESIDENCE | |
| COLOR | White | COLOR | White |
| AGE AT LAST BIRTHDAY | 31 (Years) | AGE AT LAST BIRTHDAY | 31 (Years) |
| BIRTHPLACE | Salt Lake | BIRTHPLACE | Switzerland |
| OCCUPATION | R R Engineer | OCCUPATION | |

Number of Child of this Mother 5th Number of Children of this Mother now living 5

CERTIFICATE OF ATTENDING PHYSICIAN OR MIDWIFE *

I hereby certify that I attended the birth of this child, and that it occurred on January 1 1909, at 12:19 A.M.

No Premature No or Still Birth? (Yes or No.)

* When there was no attending physician or midwife, then the father, householder, etc., should make this return.

(Signature) J S Scott
Date January 4 1909. Phy (Physician or Midwife)

Give name added from supplemental report.

Address of Physician or Midwife 11-12 Mercantile Blk

190 Filed Jan 13 1909. M R Stewart Registrar.

Registrar Registered No. C 1

PLACE OF BIRTH
County of Salt Lake
Precinct
Town or Village of
City of Salt Lake

**CERTIFICATE OF BIRTH**
STATE OF UTAH

Street and No. 476 North 3rd West
If in Hospital or other Institution, give its name instead of Street and number.

FULL NAME OF CHILD Alda Margarete Bihler (If child is not yet named, make supplemental report, as directed.)

Sex of Child Female | Twin, Triplet, or Other Single | and | Number in Order of Birth — | Legitimate? yes | Date of Birth Jan 1, 2 1909 (Month) (Day) (Year)

| FATHER | | MOTHER | |
|---|---|---|---|
| FULL NAME | Charles C Bihler | FULL MAIDEN NAME | Hannah Aldous |
| RESIDENCE | 476 No 3rd West | RESIDENCE | |
| COLOR | White | COLOR | White |
| AGE AT LAST BIRTHDAY | 33 (Years) | AGE AT LAST BIRTHDAY | 31 (Years) |
| BIRTHPLACE | Nebraska | BIRTHPLACE | Utah |
| OCCUPATION | Locomotive Engineer | OCCUPATION | |

Number of Child of this Mother 2d Number of Children of this Mother now living 2

CERTIFICATE OF ATTENDING PHYSICIAN OR MIDWIFE *

I hereby certify that I attended the birth of this child, and that it occurred on January 2 1909, at 1:35 A.M.

No Premature No or Still Birth? (Yes or No.)

* When there was no attending physician or midwife, then the father, householder, etc., should make this return.

(Signature) E E Wilcox
Date Jan 4 1909. Ph. (Physician or Midwife)

Give name added from supplemental report.

Address of Physician or Midwife 407 Templeton

190 Filed Jan, 13 1909. M R Stewart Registrar.

Registrar Registered No. C 2

**Figure 6.1a. This is an example of a birth certificate issued in Salt Lake City, Utah. Some archives have responsibility for vital records, while others decline these documents. Servicing birth and death records is often time consuming and labor intensive. Courtesy Salt Lake County Health Department.**

**Figure 6.1b.** Some local government archives collect artifacts and use them in museum exhibits. The Butte-Silver Bow Public Archives in Montana has an active program of rotating exhibits and hosting public receptions. Photo courtesy of Walter Hinick, the Montana Standard.

information benefit researchers? Constituent correspondence, generally accepted as a government record, can have permanent value but much of the subject matter is likely to be mundane requests for infrastructure repair, political opinions, and requests for autographs. Should you choose to keep constituent correspondence, consider sampling to reduce the volume.

Some non-records merit attention. Ancillary research tools such as published books on local history, hand-drawn or commercially produced maps, vertical files, and street directories are all examples of non-government records that are acceptable components of an archives research library.

## ACCESSIONING AND TRANSFER DOCUMENTATION

*Accessioning* is the practice of documenting the specific point when a body of materials or documents is received into the archives. The process involves creating a title for the materials, recording information about its volume and date span, and noting the date of the transfer, among other things. Accessioning accomplishes two things: it provides a paper trail explaining how the collection arrived at the archives, and documents the chain of ownership.

The resulting data is called an *accession record* or a *holding record*. This can also include supporting information, such as correspondence or historical background on the materials' origins.

An *accession register* can be in the form of a log that is kept in a computer spreadsheet or on paper. It usually has most basic information about a collection—when it arrived, its volume, and its accession number, a unique number that is assigned to a new incoming collection. Automated accessioning software is available and, depending upon the size of your program, can simplify the process. Accession registers are also where you would document additions to existing collections. Such documentation is valuable because it demonstrates when additions were made to the larger body of records.

Accessioning records within a local government is much different from acquiring documents from a private party. For one thing, the legal custody of the records is much less complicated since they already belong to the government. Because government records are created by a governmental unit with public funding, they are by nature public records.

There is no set or established procedure for transferring records from one department to the department responsible for the archives (city/county clerk, auditor, governing body, for example). The most widespread practice in local governments is a standardized transmittal or transfer form, which includes most of the information that goes into an accessioning record: originating department, a brief description of the subject matter, volume, and date span. If the transfer is based on records management scheduling, there should be room to note the retention number that corresponds to "permanent." Be sure that boxes transferred to archives during the review process have been stricken from the list of box control numbers in the records management schedule to prevent confusion over final disposition. For an example of a transfer form, please see appendix 2.

The next most common procedure is to transfer legal and physical custody in a written memorandum. Because records are legally the property of the creating department, both their legal and physical custody needs to be conveyed to the archives under the signature of a department head or other designated official. A transfer memorandum can include standardized language stating that the materials described become the physical and legal property of the archives' department, that the archives reserves the right to decline parts of a collection, and that the materials can be loaned for exhibition under certain conditions. There should be a space for the archives to acknowledge receipt with signature and date.

It is not uncommon for an archives to receive materials or collections without adequate accessioning or transfer documentation. In lieu of formal archives policies, some departments and well-meaning employees simply drop off boxes with a note. For collections that lack proper accession documentation, it is important to create a file that holds as many clues as can be determined about its origin. Even if it means adding a note to the holding record that acknowledges the earliest date the item was seen in the archives, some documentation is better than nothing.

If the archives operates within a non-governmental entity yet collects and cares for local government records, such as a local historical society, it is important that you have a written agreement with that government. It was not always the case, but most local governments now have laws stating that public records may not be given away to a non-governmental repository. Because some local governments do not have the space or ability to care for their own historic records, agreements are not uncommon and can work to the benefit of both parties.

Materials entering a local government archives from private hands should be accompanied by a deed of gift. Like a transfer memorandum, the letter needs to incorporate language transferring both physical and legal custody to the archives.

## ALIENATED RECORDS

Sadly, permanently valuable local government documents can often be lost, borrowed, or stolen. Especially in the absence of an archives program, local governments are vulnerable to treasure hunters and thieves who believe it is acceptable to privately possess records that belong to the public. Other times, careless recordkeeping and misfiling by staff members means records cannot be found.

Local governments have lost thousands of official historical government records, many ending up in private collections. All local governments should be deeply concerned about the number of records that appear for sale in auction catalogs and on online auction and selling websites such as eBay. The disappearance of government records into private hands deprives the public of access to important information and deprives governments of the records that were created and maintained with public funds. Because archives document government actions for the review of citizens, the inappropriate transfer of archival records into private hands greatly restricts access to them, which in turn hampers government accountability.

Records not properly scheduled or appraised for historical value sometimes find their way into other local archives, such as a public library's special collection or a local historical society. If records are transferred to another government department—like a library—they are still in governmental custody and not truly alienated. Archival documents also wind up quite innocently in the hands of local historical societies. In more than a few instances, local history groups have rescued improperly disposed of records from dumps, curbs, and private storage units. Rather than treating them like thieves, they should be commended for their good stewardship, regardless of whether they return the records or not.

Not all people who purchase local government records know they are holding stolen property. Once they are made aware, individuals sometimes resolve matters amicably by "donating" the records back to the government. Again, praise often goes a lot further than condemnation. Some collectors are generous enough to recognize thefts and purchase items with the intention of returning them to the government. There are, however, some who knowingly collect local government documents who are less likely to be so charitable. Legal recourse is the last resort for return of records, a process called *replevin*.

Replevin is the process of regaining physical and legal custody of records through lawsuit. Any legal actions will need to be initiated through the local government's legal department. To be successful, the local government must prove that the records had previously been a part of the archives, or within government control. Because manuscript dealers and collectors stand to lose money if they forfeit a document, expect a confrontation, but don't get caught up in it. Let the administrators follow the legal process and be ready to help provide evidence of government ownership when requested.

There are several possible actions and outcomes to consider for replevin. One is to begin litigation and settle the question of ownership by mutual agreement. Another is to move forward with litigation and let the court determine ownership. A third outcome is to not involve the courts and settle by mutual agreement. Perhaps the most famous case of replevin in the archives community is the state of North Carolina's reclamation of its original copy of the Bill of Rights, documented in David Howard's 2010 book *Lost Rights: The Misadventures of a Stolen American Relic*.[2]

## ARRANGEMENT AND DESCRIPTION OF LOCAL GOVERNMENT ARCHIVES

Principles of arrangement and description of government archives and records in North America trace back to three related sets of theories, each building upon their predecessor. The writings of Samuel Muller, Johan Adriaan Feith and Robert Fruin, all archivists from the Netherlands, published *Manual for the Arrangement and Description of Archives* in 1898, which established concepts of collection integrity and maintaining original order in archival records. Sir Hilary Jenkinson's *A Manual of Archival Administration* (1937) built upon the work of the Dutch archivists. His writings elaborated upon his predecessors and reinforced the belief that government records primarily serve its creators and did not anticipate citizen use of public records.[3]

T. R. Schellenberg, archivist at the U.S. National Archives, embraced some of the earlier ideas but promoted his opinion that government records should be arranged and described for the use of the public as much as for internal government employees. His seminal books *Modern Archives: Principles and Techniques* (1956) and *The Management of Archives* (1965), however much debated today, contain guidelines for the arrangement of government records that still hold much value for local government archives.

All of them believed firmly in the concept of *respect des fonds*, which asserts the priority of the governmental unit as the overarching organizing scheme and hierarchy for records series. They also all strongly believed in the cardinal rule of *original order*, which is to acknowledge and not disturb the order of the files whenever possible. Rearranging and disturbing the original order prevents understanding of the relationship of the files to their creator and destroys the context in which the files relate to one another. An imposed order is created as a last resort when original order cannot be determined.

Figure 6.2.  Not all collections arrive at a local government archives undisturbed. A few labeled folders and envelopes among these photographic materials are the only evidence of any sort of arrangement. Photo by John H. Slate, Dallas Municipal Archives, City of Dallas, TX.

## Arrangement Differences between Government Archives and Personal Papers

A contrast between the arrangement practices for personal papers and government records is a helpful way to conceptualize an approach to working with local government archives. Collections comprised of the personal papers of individuals and those of private organizations present significant intellectual puzzles to determine the original order and structure of bodies of records. People and private businesses can tailor their filing systems to their personal habits or business practices, without regard for outside users. Government operations, however, are largely standardized and their business is dependent upon forms and procedures that follow fairly logical filing schemes.

Although they were formulated for federal records, archivist T. R. Schellenberg's observations about government records generally hold true for local governments. He noted that many types of records that include repetitive actions, such as forms, recur and reappear often in files. Recurrent types are found in greater numbers in larger agencies than smaller ones, meaning there is more routine and more repetition. Schellenberg's point that archives have recurrent types of records and homogeneity means that arrangement should be able to be performed simply.[4]

Considerable time is often spent in trying to understand the idiosyncrasies of people and groups and how they affect the ways their records are arranged and ordered. This is much less so with government records. One of the most satisfying and comforting aspects of government archives is knowing that the vast majority of materials you will encounter are usually going to be predictable and understandable in their nature and arrangement.

## LEVELS OF ARRANGEMENT

Government records are best understood as being in a chain of levels of arrangement (sometimes called levels of control), from broad to specific. The archivist and theorist Oliver Wendell Holmes described levels of arrangement that start at the institutional level and end at document level. Holmes's article is essential reading for any archivist.[5]

The *institutional level* is the government itself and its major departments. In a municipal government, imagine the major departments as units—police, fire, water, public works. The next level lower is the *record group* or *subgroup*. In the example of a municipal agency, a health department will have multiple programs such as a subgroup for women and children and another subgroup for seniors. One level lower below the subgroup is the *series* level. Under the subgroup for women and children there may be further separate series for immunization, reproductive health, and adolescent health. Under each subseries is the *folder* level, such as the various files that contain information on that program. For example, under the immunization series there might be files directly relating to that activity—such as correspondence, reports, and statistical data. The lowest level is the *item* level—the document itself, the individual items that make up the contents of a folder.

Filing units or folders usually have some kind of filing structure or pattern, whether it is alphabetical, chronological, numerical, or geographical, to name just a few examples. In a police department or a sheriff's office, activity reports might be filed by service division if the city or county is divided into service districts. For the convenience of retrieval, quite a lot of local government material is found arranged chronologically; for example, a set of city codes or annual reports might be filed starting with the earliest code, ascending to the most recent code.

This is a very simplistic description of how to analyze the structure or archival records. Working through these levels to understand how the body of records is organized is essential to creating a useful description; by creating a good description, researchers will understand the nature of the materials, and how to find what they want in them. These are not hard and fast rules, only suggested guidelines for arrangement. There are many exceptions and

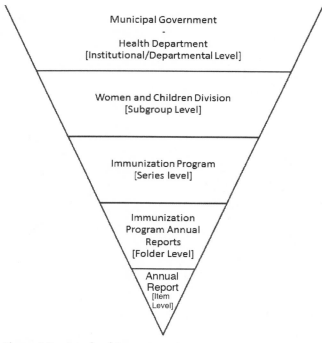

**Figure 6.3.   Levels of Arrangement.**

nuances in arrangement to consider, and archivists have to make decisions based on the records at hand.

## MORE PRODUCT, LESS PROCESS

Because it is easy to get mired in the details of arrangement, processing backlogs can grow and you may want to limit how much time is spent on this aspect of processing. Backlogs in processing collections have bedeviled archivists for decades but can be erased through the application of "minimal processing." "More Product, Less Process: Revamping Traditional Archival Processing," (MPLP for short) by Mark A. Greene and Dennis Meissner, published in 2005, is perhaps the single most significant article published on archival theory and practice in the last thirty years. The article cites the lack of productivity in archival processing and the long amount of time it typically takes to make collections available for researchers.

The article's authors prescribe a set of guidelines that have the goal of moving collections out of the processing area faster to improve access, making sure that arrangement meets a minimum baseline for being useful without being excessive, conducting minimal preservation on collections, and providing some kind of description—however simple—to make the collection more immediately useful. As Greene and Meissner state, "In other words, it is time to focus on what we absolutely need to do, instead of on all the other things we might do in a world of unbounded resources."[6] MPLP has had a major impact upon the archives world and imparts a serious lesson for local government archivists: minimal processing and arrangement gets collections out to researchers faster without compromising the materials.

## DESCRIBING ARCHIVAL RECORDS

You've got to know what you're looking at before you can use it. Collections are less valuable and harder to use if they are not properly described. Good descriptions help researchers and users understand what the collection is about, its volume, and what period of time it covers. They can be described both broadly and very specifically, the depth of detail depending upon many different factors such as time and labor. The three most common tools of description for archival materials are inventories, finding aids, and machine-readable cataloging (MARC) records.

*Inventories* are nothing more than lists of box contents. They can be created as a preliminary checklist at the beginning of processing as well as a final product. Using consistent language and vocabulary is important since researchers who may understand only a fraction of the subject matter depend upon clearly written and organized inventories to make informed decisions about what is worthwhile to investigate. Do not use acronyms or abbreviations unless you spell them out first. Not everyone, in particular researchers from other locations, understands what abbreviated terms mean.

Inventories usually list the box number and folder number, with a description of the folder's contents and date span. Series titles can be listed to show the arrangement structure, as long as they don't interfere with the flow of the box and folder number sequence.

A *finding aid* incorporates an inventory into a broader document that provides valuable information about the collection. Its component parts are a collection description, a description of the scope and content of the collection, date span, volume, and format of the material. The collection description usually includes biographical and historical information related to the collection, sometimes providing more detailed background information to offer historical context. Date spans are often expressed as inclusive dates, meaning the date of the earliest item in the collection and the date of the latest item. Inclusive dates can be misleading, so break up the dates to indicate the bulk of the materials if there are wide gaps within the larger date span.

Volume in archives is expressed in linear feet and inches, traditionally, as it measures the space taken up on a shelf rather than the depth of the materials. If your archives is a component of a records management program, you may want to measure space in cubic feet and inches to be consistent with the parent program, though cubic measurement doesn't adapt well to smaller collections under a cubic foot.

Listing the format or formats represented in the collection is useful because it may affect the researcher's ability to use the materials. For instance, in photography it is important to indicate if the materials are photographic prints, negatives, transparencies, or digital images. Prints do not require any equipment for viewing, but negatives and transparencies usually require a light table or other backlit viewing source and digital images require a computer to view. Another example is audiovisual materials. If a collection is made up of VHS videotape, it can only be viewed if the archives has a digital transfer copy of the tape or if it has reliable playback equipment.

Restrictions on use of or access to the materials is important primarily to forewarn users of preservation concerns. If a collection has very fragile material but has the information in another format, make sure it is clear to researchers that they can't handle the original but can still get to the information. Torn or damaged documents that have been photocopied, photographed, or scanned are a common example of a restriction based on preservation.

Finding aids created for the World Wide Web follow a standardized format called Encoded Archival Description (EAD). EAD is a non-proprietary standard for the encoding of finding aids for use on the Internet and use all of the previously mentioned descriptive elements and more. Descriptive standards are freely available on the web and may require some training to implement.

Machine-Readable Cataloging (MARC) for archival materials is one last form of a finding aid. Closely connected to the library community, MARC records are a cataloging record much like a record that is created for a book that is searchable in an online public access catalog. A MARC record is a summary of the more detailed information usually found in a finding aid, and is usually just a collection-level description. While MARC cataloging is useful in an archives connected to a library catalog, EAD records are gaining dominance as a preferred form of description.

## Descriptive Elements for Local Government Archives

Most of the elements of description previously mentioned can be applied across the board to any kind of records, but there is some information that is specific to local governments that should be considered in the descriptive process. This includes corporate or agency history, governmental functions, and terminology.

Corporate or agency history is an important part of a finding aid because it helps researchers understand the origins and development of a particular service or department of a local government. It is also helpful for understanding arrangement. For a collection about a county-owned hospital, it was necessary to explain why there were both municipal government and county government records within the same box. Research revealed that the entity originated as the city-county hospital, which was funded jointly. The municipal government later opted out of the management of the hospital, leaving the county as sole owner and operator. The history of the hospital helped the processing archivist maintain the city and county portions of the collection as separate series, and also provided long-forgotten information about the hospital's past.

In the city of Dallas, Texas, its municipally owned radio station started as an early form of public safety dispatch for the Dallas Fire Department. At the time of its inception in 1921, Radio Station WRR was built and later licensed to provide communication between the central fire department station and the rest of the city's stations. As the radio station reached its eighty-fifth year of service, it was able to explain its origins and reason for existence.

In a third example, a collection regarding building inspection contained conflicting information about its parent department. Research helped discover that the office had been placed under the administration of no less than four departments in its one-hundred-year history. The processing archivist was then able to see evidence of multiple series, and ensure the arrangement of the records reflected the department's tangled administrative history.

Governmental functions also need to be explained to researchers through finding aids. Citizens sometimes do not know how a department operates or understand its functions and responsibilities. An example is a county elections department. Elections involve a cycle that must follow state and sometimes federal election law, requiring the governing body to follow a calendar that may initiate more than a year before the actual election day. The outcomes of elections involve a canvass report, which aggregates voting data to determine winners. If the elections process has changed significantly over time, that is also a good thing to describe. Brief explanations of common governmental practices prepare researchers for the kinds of records they will find within a collection.

Terminology is a third area that is important in the descriptive process. Water engineering, for example, is a scientific endeavor which has its own language and terms. While you don't want to overwhelm or confuse researchers, you still must organize records according to their functions. Users must see the difference between a pump station and a water purification plant, and between a purification plant and a wastewater treatment plant. Similarly it is useful to help researchers understand terms used in such areas as surveying; in courts; in planning and zoning; and in transportation.

A wider discussion of arrangement and description principles and theory can be found in Kathleen D. Roe's book *Arranging and Describing Archives and Manuscripts* published by the Society of American Archivists.

## NOTES

1. Frank Boles, *Selecting and Appraising Archives and Manuscripts* (Chicago: Society of American Archivists, 2005), 11–12.

2. Ellen Mattern, "The Replevin Process in Government Archives: Recovery and the Contentious Question of Ownership" (PhD dissertation, University of Pittsburgh, 2014), 61, 227.

3. Frederic Miller, *Arranging and Describing Archives and Manuscripts* (Chicago: Society of American Archivists, 1990), 20–21.

4. T. R. Schellenberg, *Modern Archives: Principles and Techniques* (Chicago: University of Chicago Press), 96–97.

5. Oliver Wendell Holmes, "Archival Arrangement—Five Different Operations at Five Different Levels," *American Archivist* 27, no. 1 (January, 1964): 21–41.

6. Mark Greene and Dennis Meissner, "More Product, Less Process: Revamping Traditional Archival Processing," *American Archivist* 68, no. 2 (Fall/Winter 2005): 212–13.

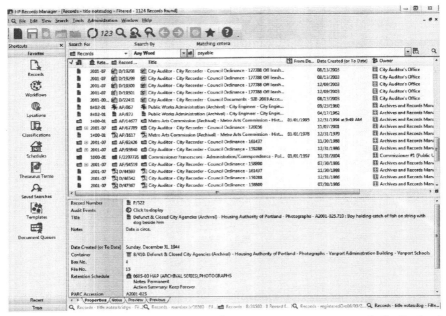

Figure 7.1.   A screen shot of an electronic document management system in the Portland City Archives in Oregon. Permanent electronic records share many of the same characteristics of paper-based archives. Courtesy City of Portland Archives & Records Center.

# 7

# Electronic Records in Local Government Archives

In an ever-changing information environment, electronic records are an important component of any local government archives. This chapter discusses very basic concepts for managing electronic records and documents of permanent and long-term value, understanding that best practices and recommendations are gaining consensus while technologies for file storage and retrieval are continually evolving. Each local government settles on its own definitions, but a common description of what constitutes an electronic record is any information that is recorded in a form of computer processing and that satisfies the definition of a local government record in the local government's code.

Managing electronic records with permanent value in a local government archives is important to the day-to-day operations and accountability of governments. They must be protected and accessible. Local, state, and federal laws often prescribe what kinds of electronic records are to be kept permanently in a record retention schedule, but other items are not as clearly identified for their enduring value. The archivist's role in managing permanently valuable electronic records is to help establish policy and work with the government's information professionals and records management professionals (if there are any) to ensure the long-term preservation of these records.

An important thing to remember about scanned and digitized electronic records is that they should be treated with the same care you treat originals. In most cases they do not replace original items, nor should they be used as an excuse to destroy originals. However, in the case of analog audio transferred to digital, the digital copy is replacing the analog original because the ability to play magnetic tape is dying.

While digital surrogates may decrease handling of originals, they should be viewed more as an access tool, in that they may be shared and manipulated easily. For example, a scanned image of an oversized map or architectural drawing vastly improves access to an item that can be unwieldy due to size, or have preservation issues such as tearing or creasing, or may have legibility issues. The mitigation of these concerns, not to mention the ease of sharing, does not absolve the archivist from the care of the original.

## ELECTRONIC RECORDS POLICIES

Some, but not all, local governments have established electronic records policies. These policies are usually agreed upon by stakeholders in a government through a committee. Common stakeholders might include an administrative unit, the legal unit, records management, information technology departments and personnel, archivists, and librarians, plus input from various departments with specialized needs. If you are in a local government with few policies or oversight on electronic records in place, you may be able to draft polices based on best practices found in other local governments nearby or in other states. Some state archives include electronic records as a part of their local government records program assistance. Regional universities with electronic records programs are also a valuable resource. The professional literature on this subject area is expanding, and there are a number of good books with helpful information, such as *Effective Approaches for Managing Electronic Records and Archives* (Bruce Dearstyne, editor, Scarecrow Press, 2002).

There are three basic areas of knowledge an archivist should understand about electronic records—the initial control of records, their continuing control (policy and oversight), and their sustainability.

## INITIAL CONTROL

### Inventory of Records

Just as you would conduct a preliminary inventory of paper documents in records management or in an archives, it is important to grasp the "big picture" of how much and what types of records you have. Inventory sheets may include fields that identify the department that created the records, some kind of title to describe the records, and a date span (creation dates of the earliest and most recent items). An inventory sheet also usually includes a series description, which is a sentence or two that describes the content; an indication of the arrangement of the records (alphabetical, numerical, chronological, alphanumeric, or no arrangement); retention notes from the records management officer; and its present location and quantity. Inventory forms may include some, all, or even more of these information fields.

## Inventory of Records and Information Systems

Almost as important as tracking the records themselves is knowing what kind of system your electronic information is stored in and how it operates. Are permanently valuable files maintained on secure servers that can't be altered or deleted by other employees? Are files stored in unstable storage formats such as compact disks and flash drives, or worse, are they on obsolete storage formats such as floppy disks? You don't have to be an expert on electronic storage systems, but you do need to be able to communicate with your information technology professionals to know where the electronic archives materials will be stored, where to find information on how that system operates (commonly called system documentation), how it is backed up, and how information on that system will be migrated forward in the future.

Some local governments use a centralized document management system, in which all departments share documents in a common area. The system automates the tracking, management, and storage of documents through programmed actions. At the point of creation, the person who starts a new document will be required to create tracking information or metadata that can be used by the tracking system later on. Similarly, a retention date can be automatically applied to a certain class of documents so that they will be flagged for review when their end date arrives. Document management is a useful tool in identifying records with archival value, and for making them available once tagged as permanent. However, these systems are not usually designed for long-term preservation of records and those records will need to be moved to a preservation system just like paper records are transferred to the archives.

## Creation or Modification of Records Schedules

If your local government has an active records management program, they likely have records schedules that will apply to electronic records. Many governments utilize existing schedules created by state government local records programs. Local government officials often take the same schedules and modify them to fit their government's needs. For instance, local laws may extend the retention period for certain classes of documents if they are required to be kept for continuing cases of litigation.

Even if schedules for paper documents are used for electronic records, you need to account for the actual electronic form. For example, audiotape, videotape, compact disks, and reel-to-reel audio might be more properly termed generically as "recordings."

## Archival Appraisal of Electronic Records

The appraisal and disposition of electronic records is generally the same as actions taken on paper records. Electronic documents having permanent value are eligible for transfer to the archives if they have either passed the appraisal process for records which have reached the end of their retention period, or have been designated as permanent at their point of creation. During their retention period, the documents usually must be retained in their native (original) format and be retrievable and unaltered. Following transfer to the archives, some electronic documents may be printed out and maintained as hard copy or converted to a more stable file format such as PDF, but keeping them in their native format is usually preferred whenever possible.

The appraisal process involves an analysis of value to determine if a record has permanent value. Common values examined include evidential value (what does the document tell us about the government and how it works?); informational value (what kinds of facts does it reveal about the government, its citizens, or its clients?); legal value (what is its value to the local government for legal matters?); historical value (what does the document add to the historical record?); fiscal value (is the document valuable for conducting business?); and administrative value (does the document aid the government's operations?).

In addition to the traditional values you would apply to any record, you must also look at several very specific issues directly affecting the permanent preservation of electronic records. For instance, you'll need to weigh the benefits of preservation against its costs. If you have a collection of digital photography that takes up a great deal of server space, are you prepared and capable of maintaining that volume of material? Also you will need to look at storage, backup, software, and programming needs. In another example, if you accept GIS (geographical information systems) files, will you be able to afford the licenses for the proprietary software necessary to open and view the files? Do you have a migration strategy to convert the existing format to another format in the future? The last thing you want to do is to take on files that will be useless if you cannot open or view them.

## Drafts versus Final Versions

The records management field provides a good lesson in government record keeping. In the appraisal of electronic documents, the final version of a report or study should be considered the definitive version of that document, rather than the drafts leading up to it. In other words, save the final version, not the drafts. In the literary manuscript archives tradition, drafts are worth saving because they show evidence of the creative process in writing. However, drafts in local government records are far less valuable because they may contain factual errors or may not reflect the most complete expression of a government action or policy.

## Digital Archives Planning

If your local government does not already have a digital archives program, you may wish to explore the possibility of starting one. Because a formal program involves costs like labor and equipment, you'll want to craft a written plan that explains to administrators and governing bodies how you intend to achieve your goals. You'll need to include a full justification that clearly states purpose and objectives, and explains why preserving historic electronic information is important to the government, as well as its benefits to government business. Your planning document should also have an implementation plan that describes who will be involved, what resources you will need, where the program will be housed, and most importantly, how much it will all cost. In particular, don't just quote costs for the start-up of the program; you'll be asked immediately how much it is expected to cost per year approximately, and how you plan to sustain it into the future.

More than anything else, your greatest challenge is and may always be storage. Digital video, audio, and images in particular can be very large files. Redundancy, or creating multiple copies of files for preservation, is another matter that exponentially increases storage needs. Many electronic archives, for instance, mandate having a minimum of two or three copies of each item. Although the costs of storage may decrease over time, your basic need for more storage capacity will never stop.

## CONTINUING CONTROL (POLICY AND OVERSIGHT)

### Records Security

An electronic records security program for a local government archives should do several things. It should ensure that only authorized personnel have access to electronic records and should provide for backup and recovery of records to protect against information loss. It should also work to minimize the risk of unauthorized alteration or erasure of electronic records, whether accidental or intentional. Much of the security of your electronic records may be handled by the IT professionals within your government, though you'll want to cultivate good relations with them and discuss what kinds of options you have for security.

Hazards to electronic records are both virtual and physical—flood and fire, hard drive failure, viruses, and hacking. For physical security, storage areas for servers and other hardware should have alarm systems. For virtual security, backup plans, firewalls, and offsite data storage are vital tools for defense and recovery in the event of disaster. Disaster planning and recovery is usually coordinated through internal governmental support services, as well as through local emergency management networks. In any case, you will want to have some kind of written disaster and recovery plan for electronic data that is updated periodically.

### Maintenance and Migration Strategies for Electronic Media

Part of the preservation process for electronic media involves testing and verification of the integrity of the files. If you plan on storing your files on magnetic computer tapes, the tape mechanism should be tested several times before use. Pretesting of tapes is usually not necessary if an automated system is used that monitors read/write errors and there is a procedure in place for correcting errors.

Many digital archives programs integrate a *checksum* function into their maintenance procedures to verify file integrity or alteration. Checksum information is generated during transmission or storage of electronic files, in which a code or set of numbers can be read and compared to ensure the file was transmitted correctly and that the file has not been adversely changed. If the checksum numbers don't match, then the file has changed. Many different automated programs can now perform various types of checksums to validate file integrity, as well as to detect possible tampering. This is important for long-term storage as well. As computer media deteriorates, individual bits of a file could be lost even if the overall system is still functioning, a process called "bit rot." Checksums help monitor for change in files over time.

Sampling is another way to examine digital media for file integrity. Random sampling of all magnetic computer tapes should be read annually to identify any loss of data and to discover and correct the causes of data loss. A 10 percent sample or a sample size of fifty tapes is considered acceptable. Tapes having unrecoverable errors should be replaced if possible. Tapes damaged from other sources, such as low-quality tape, high usage, poor environment, improper handling, should be reviewed and corrected.

Because of changing technology or media deterioration, it is necessary to convert electronic storage media periodically to provide compatibility with current hardware and software. There are several ways to do this. One method is to set a schedule to recopy to the newer electronic media, or transfer data from an obsolete technology to a supportable technology. Another method, somewhat harder to achieve, is to provide backward system compatibility to the data in the older system, or to convert data to media that the system upgrade replacement can support.

## Records Storage Standards

Storing electronic records includes its physical storage on backup equipment. You'll want to make sure that storage areas meet recognized environmental control standards wherever digital media is stored—offsite or onsite. For magnetic media, the temperature should be 65–75 degrees Fahrenheit, and 30–50 percent relative humidity; separately controlled temperature is ideal.[1]

## Digital Imaging Guidelines and Standards

Digitization, more generally referred to as scanning, should be done to internationally recognized standards wherever possible. Adhering to standards will pay off in the long run and help avoid having to rescan and handle fragile items. There are different standards for scanning textual material and images. In text scanning, your goal is legibility. In image scanning, you want to create a digital file that as accurately as possible reproduces the colors and tonal range of the original.

There are many recommendations for how best to scan, but a few very elementary suggestions are offered here. At a minimum, always scan at 100 percent of your original size. If you create a file that is 100 percent or larger of the original at print out, you can always make access copies, sometimes called derivatives, that are smaller and easier to use for some purposes. For instance, thumbnails, postage stamp–size scanned images, may be acceptable for use on a website or quick reference, but you'll have very poor, heavily pixilated images if you attempt to print out at a larger size. There are other factors to consider in scanning, such as bit depth and resolution Bit depth corresponds to the richness of color; 24-bit color is considered "true color." Resolution is a measure of the amount of detail in an image.

Standardized file formats and consistent file-naming conventions are another part of standardization. To date, the most stable file format for images is the TIFF. TIFFs can be saved as uncompressed files, which is important in preserving the quality of the image. Derivatives or smaller versions of original files are well suited to the JPG format, which is compressed. A compressed file is smaller and can be sent easily as an e-mail attachment. GIF files are good to use on websites because they are usually small and load quickly.

Every new scanned item must have a file name. To ensure efficient storage and retrieval, it's important to settle upon a system that is easy to follow and expand as you add more files.

Numeric and alphanumeric file names can be tied to specific collections and record groups, as well as identifying location down to box and folder level. Other naming conventions may be unique to the repository. Whichever scheme you decide upon, stick to it and avoid inconsistency.

The National Archives and the Library of Congress, as well as a number of standards and imaging organizations, have established guidelines, best practices, and standards that are used by archival institutions large and small. They are all well worth reviewing.[2]

## E-mail Management

The vast majority of e-mail messages flowing through a local government have very low informational value and do not merit permanent preservation. Think of what percentage of e-mail is valuable (signing off on a project; administrative orders), compared to the amount that has low value ("Do you want to go to lunch?"). The percentage of valuable e-mail must be maintained for specific periods of time according to records management schedules and later disposed; the remainder becomes permanent.

The decision-making level of the message is a major determinant of the value of the information content. If the correspondence involves an executive, the higher level of decision making is likely more valuable than decisions made by lower-level employees. Subject matter is another factor in deciding what to save. For example, the e-mail generated by a historic event such as the September 11, 2001, terrorist attacks is worth reviewing because it may give insight into how a local government responded locally to an event affecting the entire nation.

Local government policies and procedures for permanent records should be agreed upon by the government's information professionals, records management staff, as well as archives staff, to ensure compliance with local laws, state open records statutes, and discovery in litigation.

Ultimately, many electronic records professionals believe that the key to efficient management of e-mail messages is to train staff early on to file their work carefully and logically. Well-identified and organized information is easier to search and retrieve, and will save time and funds in the long run.

## Managing Structured Data (Databases, Spreadsheets, GIS)

In addition to all the textual and visual information managed in a local government archives, there is the type of record termed structured data.

Structured data is raw information that is used by government employees in carrying out their business and displayed in a form they can analyze, such as spreadsheets, relational databases, and layered geographical mapping information. Spreadsheet programs such as Excel help organize large amounts of information and make it possible to reorder that information in many different ways. Spreadsheets can also be used as a basis for creating graphs and charts to make a visual representation of the data.

Database management systems are another form of structured data. Programs such as Access and FileMaker, among a large field of relational database systems, operate much like spreadsheets and sort tables according to commands. Relational databases are especially useful in creating catalogs, indexes, and tracking systems.

Yet another form of structured data is geographic information systems, or GIS, which creates, manages, and manipulates geographical and other kinds of related data. In local governments it is used most often for engineering and planning and is used to map and examine such critical issues as boundaries, transportation alignment, and safety.

Unquestionably the information in a structured database has value, sometimes permanent value. In most cases, the database systems are proprietary software, meaning you must purchase specific software and/or a license in order to view or alter it. Saving data sets created in proprietary software is meaningless unless you have either reliable open-source software that you can use into the future, or your government has committed to keeping software licenses up to date. Some proprietary software, such as Adobe products, is committed to long-term access with free viewers, though you are expected to license the editing software. Even then, if the software is no longer produced or supported in the future, the chances of being able to open a file, much less manipulate it, are slim.

Some structured data, such as maps produced in GIS software, can be printed out into the PDF format for long-term preservation. Although it creates a static image, it's at least a representation of the original. It's a gamble, but it is worth saving permanently valuable structured data in formats that are predicted to be readable or supported.

## Web Content Management

Your local government may be large and have a robust and complex website, or it may be small and have only a very simple presence on the World Wide Web. Local government sub-units and departments often have web pages subordinate to a larger website for the governmental entity. They may contain static information that rarely changes, such as directional information or office hours, but they also often contain data having permanent value. Governing body rosters and election-related information, including canvass reports and vote tallies, are essential data that can change from year to year, meaning that older information gets discarded as new information is updated on the website.

Preserving web pages from local government involves using an automated tool called a web crawler to visit and revisit a specific website and preserve as much of the look of the page as possible, including pages linked to it. Archivists do face challenges in preserving websites, such as defining the scope of crawl (what are the boundaries of the site? How many external links are allowed?).

There are presently several approaches to web content capture and preservation, but few actual standards in place. A number of nonprofit international groups (such as the International Internet Preservation Consortium and the Internet Archive), and hosted services such as Archive-It and large archival repositories are actively developing standardized methods of website capture and presentation. These digital libraries are poised to change the way electronic data is collected and shared, and are already impacting the future of local government records with long-term value.

## SUSTAINABILITY

The third area of electronic records to consider is sustainability. How do you plan to make electronic records available into the future? The largest challenges are technical obsolescence and sustainable funding. Because technology changes quickly, it's important to look at several tasks that will be ongoing once you implement an electronic archives program. One is to refresh data by copying it periodically onto the same media, or to migrate it into a newer file format.

Funding is always subject to the budgetary process in local governments, as are the demands for storage, which is always growing. Planning that includes growth projections for storage as well as cost estimations is a wise way to instill confidence in funders and make yourself more aware of future needs.

There is also the prospect of copying out the information into an older or more stable format such as paper and, for text-based documents and photos, microfilm. An example is digital photography, which is especially vulnerable. Because of concerns for the long-term preservation of digital photography, some experts recommend printing out files to improve the chances of image permanence. The concept is simple: if the file becomes corrupted, a first-generation print can become its backup. Print-out onto photographic paper as backup can be a costly endeavor, however.

To become fully successful in operating an electronic records archives, it is vital that staff in charge of electronic information stay up to date on methods and tools for preservation. It is a continuous learning process. Archivists must be prepared for a significant time investment.

## NOTES

1. Minnesota Historical Society, *Electronic Records Management Guidelines—Digital Storage*, accessed October 27, 2015, http://www.mnhs.org/preserve/records/electronicrecords/erstorage.php#guidelines.

2. State Archives Department, Minnesota Historical Society Digital Imaging March 2004, Version 4.

# 8

# Local Government Archives Reference

In *A Glossary of Archival and Records Terminology*, author Richard Pearce-Moses defines reference as "a service to aid patrons in locating materials relevant to their interests." The concept of reference generally derives from professional librarianship, in which librarians use their skills to help users find the books they desire. In the same manner, archivists and caretakers of archives must provide assistance to their users in the form of instructing them in how to develop strategies for identifying and locating collections and items within collections, offer instruction in the proper handling of archival materials, perform or take orders for reproductions, and supervise users as they examine the materials.

Local government archives are valued documents, but they are seldom so important that they should always be restricted from use. By their very nature, public records must be open to researchers in accordance with state and local laws. With few legally protected exceptions, all local government records must be open to public inspection. Many states and local governments have even codified the openness of public records as a mandate to ensure transparency and accountability. Records closed to the public are restricted for very specific reasons and generally for defined periods of time. For instance, current records of open and ongoing investigations by police departments are not considered to be archival records and are often closed to the public until investigations are complete. In other cases, fragile original items may be restricted due to preservation concerns, though copies in scanned or microfilmed form can be made available for public use while the original is protected.

Aside from the preservation and description of archival materials, reference and access is perhaps the most important role an archivist can play. To be sure, there are many important functions and tasks within an archives, but few are as satisfying as witnessing the resulting value of information to the user. A local business may save several thousand dollars thanks to the existence of a detailed building plan filed with a building permit. An attorney may be impressed when a hundred-year-old court case about a piece of land is found within fifteen minutes of her arrival at the archives. A government in a neighboring state may be able to sentence a criminal when local court records are used to prove earlier convictions for similar crimes. A family from a distant state may be able to find their slave ancestor mentioned in pre-1865 property records. This human element of having records used for a wide variety of purposes reminds staff at local government archives and at local governments themselves why the records are being saved. There are countless examples of how archival reference helps connect users with the materials they need.

## REFERENCE STAFF

Historically, local government archives usually have limited staff. The same staff members have to help access new records, describe materials for finding aids, and help researchers. All of these jobs are important but reference staff is critical to the long-term success of the archives. As Mary Jo Pugh states in *Providing Reference Service*, "No matter what pattern or combination of patterns is employed, service to users must be the foundation of all archival programs. It is critical to staff the reference desk with people capable of meeting both the intellectual and personal needs of users . . . a real dedication to public service, however, is especially vital for reference staff, whether professional, paraprofessional, or clerical."[1]

The reference staff must be familiar enough with the holdings of the archives to be able to help the person who knows what information they want, but has no idea how to find it. Staff must also consider alternative sources of information since government records will have many uses in addition to those that they were created for. For instance, wills and estate records show the division of property at the end of a person's life. These same estate records may help document the existence of slavery in a community when wills record the fact that named slaves are passed from one generation to another. The wills might also explain the development of a major subdivision that happened when an adult child divided the family property.

Clerical staff and even volunteers or student interns may be able to assist researchers with simple requests. Basic factual information about the government found in such things as spreadsheets of elected officials' terms, chronologies or "timelines" of important events in the government's history, and even organizational charts can provide clues and help narrow down the focus of research quickly. Memorization of dates and names is much less important than being able to use informational tools to help users decide what they do or do not want. From there it is important for reference staff to become familiar with the different types of documents (ledgers, minutes, annual reports, studies, interdepartmental correspondence) and the kinds of information they contain, as well as how to read and understand the components of a finding aid or inventory. To avoid becoming a research service, reference staff must make every attempt to educate users about inventories, indexes, and any kind of access tool that may aid their research. As a result of proper education, users are empowered and are less likely to eat up valuable staff time.

Paraprofessionals or professionals with more extensive knowledge of the government will be needed for more complex requests. A reference archivist should prepare for requests that may involve a variety of kinds of records. For example, a genealogist who knows their family member was in the area at a particular time but is having trouble proving their movements may want to examine a variety of records from a specific time span to see if they can find their ancestor. They may want to look at indexes and actual deed records, tax digests, estate settlements, and civil and criminal court documents. So staff should be ready to help them and broadly consider various possibilities.

## PROVIDING PHYSICAL ACCESS TO RECORDS

Good reference services take into account physical space or facilities, staffing, written policies and procedures, and access tools. One size does not always fit all, so each of these areas should be tailored to the needs and constraints of the archives and balanced with the needs of the users. A reference area, sometimes called a reading room, needs to be a clean area that is dust free and has one or more tables where users can comfortably handle materials. Reference areas work best when they are separated from other activities of a local government archives or records center. Whenever possible, the area should be free of noise and distraction to allow researchers the benefit of peace and quiet to focus on their research.

A research area should have good lighting so researchers can adequately see the materials. Both artificial and natural light are permissible, but each presents its own problems. Fluorescent lights, for example, should be filtered for harmful ultraviolet light. Natural light from windows should also be filtered via window treatments, as sunlight is another source of ultraviolet light. LED lighting is an excellent alternative light source that produces almost no ultraviolet emissions and gives off very little radiant heat. LED lights can be more expensive than traditional lighting, but the bulbs last much longer and are more energy efficient than other lighting means.

A good reference desk is equipped with a number of essential and inexpensive items to aid the researcher. Pencils should always be available to users for note taking, especially if the person forgets to bring their own or mistakenly brings an ink pen. Scratch paper or standard 8.5 x 11 note paper should be provided, even if your policies permit the use of laptop computers or tablets. The use of providing colored paper for note taking is an easy way to ensure that original documents, usually on white paper, are not carried off by researchers, either intentionally or unintentionally.

The user tables in the reference area should be clean and non-abrasive to protect the records while in use. Tables should be large enough to accommodate standardized boxes, though at least one larger table should be available to accommodate oversized maps, architectural and engineering plans and drawings, and other large unwieldy items such as ledgers or printed oversized ephemera. Because local government archives are operated within public spaces, they must abide by Americans with Disabilities Act (ADA) guidelines, which prescribe the amount of clearance needed for wheelchair access and table height, among other things.[2] It is always a good idea to have an electrical outlet within reach for the use of a portable light box/light table for viewing photographic negatives and transparencies, as well as to supply electricity for computer users, assuming policies permit. You may also want to have a library of standard reference books and files with frequently asked questions and topics for your area available. Having ready-reference files and basic information handy makes it easy to check to see who was mayor in 1870, or when a historic school building burned.

## SECURITY

Security is a major concern for reference areas. It should be a goal of every archives, regardless of size, to ensure that documents are protected from theft. An area with limited entry and exit points is important; tables should be within eyesight of the reference staff for security, preferably segregated from work areas. Staff should be stationed at a desk where boxes may be requested and retrieved, with adjacent shelving or carts which can serve as a holding area for both boxes that are in use as well as boxes that have been used and await reshelving.

When an archives is the only tenant in a building, there is a tendency to locate the reference area near the front door so that users can get in and out quickly and easily. This perceived convenience in layout can have major drawbacks. It is better to maintain a reception area/security checkpoint near the entry to prevent theft, but also to remind researchers that they are entering an area that is being monitored. Establishing clear boundaries in an archives can mean the difference between being helpful and letting researchers "help themselves."

A research area is most secure when a staff member can see the entire area at all times. Whenever possible, an area free of structural columns or other impediments to oversight improves the odds of preventing theft. Security cameras with a monitor visible to staff can be helpful if you can afford them and they are appropriate for your space. Should the reference area be extremely busy with multiple researchers, additional staff may be called in to help in providing reference service and monitoring researchers. You should definitely consider having lockers or "cubby holes" for belongings and a coat rack for coats and umbrellas; most archives permit only materials needed for actually doing research inside the research area.

A research area requires constant supervision and depends heavily upon the staffing level. The archivist or person in charge of reference will need a staff member to retrieve needed items, or conversely, a staff member can be posted in the reference and research area while the archivist pulls requests. Archivists

**Figure 8.1.** A reception desk is often the first thing researchers see upon entering an archives. Users are required to register and learn about archives policies and procedures before entering. Courtesy City of Portland Archives & Records Center.

Figure 8.2.  Reading rooms and research areas in local government archives typically have large tables so that researchers have ample space to use records. Courtesy City of Portland Archives & Records Center.

**Figure 8.3.** The reference desk in the background has an unobstructed view of all users and research desks. Courtesy City of Portland Archives & Records Center.

must not leave a reading room with individuals looking at original documents unattended. If another staff member is not available to supervise the reading room, the requestor may be asked to come back at a later time when the materials will be available. Some archives will pull original materials upon request, while others set a specific time to pull items—perhaps twice a day—at such times as 9 AM and 1:30 PM. In some cases, the reference area may be entirely closed during the noon hour and the room cleared. Signage or written policy should be visible to researchers to inform them of the archives' retrieval practices and to avoid lengthy waits or having to schedule additional time.

## TYPES OF RESEARCHERS

Local government archives have several distinctive types of researchers. Every researcher is different, but there are some generalizations that are helpful to understanding reference needs. Some know exactly what they want, while others may have no idea at all. Regardless, any archives that prides itself on customer service should endeavor to help both those who need little assistance, as well as those who sometimes require some hand-holding. Everyone deserves to be treated with respect, no matter the question or manner in which it is communicated.

Users of local government archives can be neatly broken down into two groups: internal and external. The ratio of internal users to outside users in local governments is often heavily weighted toward the internal—government employees and elected officials of the local government are generally considered the most frequent users of a local archives. Government staff and members of boards and commissions often need archival materials to perform their jobs. For example, questions of policy precedent come up often, requiring access to older minutes, maps, legal records, and files. Law enforcement agencies may need older criminal court records to guide a judge in determining proper sentencing for an offender.

On the external side, locally based citizens form another major group of users of local government archives. Locals have a wide variety of reasons for needing access to local records. They may require access to a deed to settle a challenge to an estate, or they may need to make sure their property boundaries are protected and documented when a neighbor infringes upon their land. Some of the most basic functions of life often require use of archives or documents of permanent value. Citizens frequently must use court records to prove they were granted a divorce before remarrying, or to clarify property ownership in the settlement that officially ended the marriage.

Employees of other governments constitute another set of users of local government archives. Another government may be located in a neighboring city just a few miles away, or the government could be several states away. Frequently records are requested for purposes of comparison. For instance, sentencing records for criminal court cases may be consulted if the requesting government is in a state that gives either harsher or more lenient sentences. States that have a "three-strikes" sentencing law are an acute example, in which archival records of superior or trial courts are essential to proving that a person was sentenced for the same crime, frequently a felony.

Historians and genealogists are another class of user of local government records. These researchers check deed and estate records to determine where family members lived in earlier centuries and what possessions they owned. They also look at marriage applications to see if the parents of the married couples are listed. Industrious researchers also study court records and their indexes to locate ancestors. Historians use a wide variety of local government archives for academic research, including tax records, planning studies and reports, board and commission minutes, plats, maps, photographs, and law enforcement materials.

A last group of government archives users is students. While serious research may be mostly the purview of high school, undergraduate, and graduate students, students of any age should be encouraged to use primary sources. It is never too early to introduce archives to a locality's future tax payers and decision makers. Reference work with these researchers is often enhanced through the archives' support of National History Day contests, Daughters of the American Revolution essay contests, or state and local history observances. When working with students, staff may need to take extra time to explain materials and extra staffing may be needed to assist and supervise younger users when entire classes visit. Archives may make reproductions of some of the records available for the students. For instance, teenagers doing a history day presentation may use digital surrogates of minute books in lieu of originals. What's most important to remember is that first experiences leave important first impressions. Early exposure to historical documents helps cultivate respect for and interest in local government and local history.

## THE REFERENCE INTERVIEW

Good reference work is an art. It starts with the reference interview, which is the act of learning what users want; communicating their needs to staff; and explaining to users in return what the archives may or may not have on a given subject or topic. When people come to the archives or make queries through electronic mail, they will need to identify themselves and indicate their subject of interest. This information can be as simple as name and e-mail address. For in-person researchers, a visitor log is the first thing they will see at check-in. A log or visitor record may request all or some of the following information: full name, phone number, e-mail address, physical address, research topic, and reason for research.

The reference process is one of human interaction. A government official or a private citizen needs particular information, and the job of the archivist is to help determine where the information is, and to get the materials into the hands of the individual. This dialogue can take place in person, or over e-mail, by text message, telephone, or mail. The interview process is often easiest if it takes place in person. The discussion between the two parties can help the archivist determine what is being sought. Start by asking simple questions and try to quickly get to the point. Try to keep the discussion on track as it can become nebulous. An excited historian or genealogist may want to share everything they know before they ever explain why they are at your doorstep or sending you a query. Since initial queries can often be vague, try to help narrow down whatever dates or facts the person can share and build subsequent questions upon them.

Interviews via electronic mail, US mail or telephone may require more time to zero in on the details. If one party is not clear with their questions or answers, follow up is necessary. However, a major advantage of communicating in advance of a meeting is that the archivist has time to identify relevant records and retrieve them and have them ready for the person when they arrive, thus saving time for the researcher and enabling the archivist more latitude to pull records when convenient. Either way, the goal is to help the researcher to find the information she needs, to recommend another archives to find the materials, or to help her realize the materials she seeks might not exist.

Reference questions may be very simple if a person needs a specific record. For instance, if someone is seeking to document the marriage of their grandparents, they may know immediately they need the marriage license and application. They may come in knowing the actual date of the marriage and the reference archivist simply retrieves the marriage files or register for that particular date.

Other topics are more complex and may require more detailed questioning. A government official or a graduate student working on a major paper may seek records from a defunct water authority in a small town. They may need correspondence, final reports from a state or federal grant, photographs, and maps and charts. Gathering all of these materials may be time consuming and involved. The requestor may have to schedule one time to look at the materials, or may have to schedule follow-up visits if the materials are voluminous.

As a local government archivist you may often have to make judgment calls on the amount of time you can spend trying to help a researcher and the depth of research you can do for one person. Your archives will probably have a maximum amount of time you can spend assisting one person. Multiple researchers and research questions can require a lot of time. A beginning genealogist or a middle school student who is not familiar with doing research may want you to provide detailed help. Another person may want you to transcribe the seventeenth-century handwriting on a document for them. Others may want your help determining square footage from building plans or figuring out exactly where a property described in a deed record is located. You and your archives will be well served if you know in advance how much time you can spend to assist people in using records. A general guideline could be spending ten minutes for in-person inquiries, fifteen minutes for e-mail and telephone inquiries, and twenty minutes for correspondence.[3] A small archives may have more time to spend with researchers than this and a slow day may mean you have more time, but making a policy on time and adhering to it will ensure fairness to researchers, especially on a busy day when many requests seem to come in all at once.

Archivists must also accept the reality that no record may exist in your holding for a query. You will sometimes have to send the researcher to other facilities if it is believed the information can be found elsewhere. Some topics that appear to be local government issues are actually local and state issues and may be documented at both levels. For instance, more information about industrial development in an area may be found in the records of a local business development authority rather than a local government. Documentation of manufacturing plants may be found at both local and state levels. Newspaper stories, plats, and early site photographs may be found with local governments, while official records granting tax abatements may be part of the files of the state economic development office or another agency. The reference archivist must be ready to suggest where else to look.

Finally, many people come to local government archives seeking records that were never created in that locality, lack comprehensiveness, or may not be considered a government record. One city may have detailed building plans and maps that date back to 1800 or earlier that assist homeowners in the twenty-first century in planning for renovations. A neighboring municipality may only have building plans that date back to 1970 or 1980. Similar issues exist with photographic documentation. Some archives will have an abundance of photographs. The thoroughness of documentation will vary from department to department, and from decade to decade. A long-serving mayor with an agenda for local history or a public works department that conducted intensive self-documentation may have extensive files of every civic activity, including road and sewer building projects and streetscape beautifications.

## ACCESS POLICIES

When records are used in an archives, no matter what size, written policies on the use of archival documents is a must. To avoid any misunderstandings or misinterpretations of your house rules, always have a written set of policies, usually not longer than one to two pages, which outline your expectations of researchers and what they can expect of you. Because policies about access to government records vary by record, institution, and state, it behooves your institution to spell out exactly what you do allow and what you don't. The following policy rules are found in many archives. Many of them are common sense:

1. Briefcases, notebooks, binders, notepads, bags, purses, and other personal property are not permitted in the proximity of archives materials. These items will be secured at the service desk during your visit.
2. Researchers may take only loose sheets of notepaper or notecards into the research area. Sheets of paper are available from the archivist. Materials taken from the research area may be checked prior to the researcher's departure.
3. Pencils only may be used in the proximity of archival materials. Ink pens of any kind are prohibited. Personal computers may be used. If you need a power source, please consult the archivist.
4. Archives materials must be handled with great care, as follows:
   a. Make no marks, erasures, or any other changes to the documents.
   b. Keep all items on the table while being used. Place nothing in the lap or propped against the table.
   c. Place nothing on top of archives materials; do not write on top of, alter, lean on, fold anew, or trace materials.
   d. Turn pages slowly and carefully, touching only the margins if possible.
   e. Wear the gloves provided when working with photographic materials.
   f. Remove materials from boxes and open folders to use documents or to insert photoduplication sheets.
   g. Keep collections in their existing order and arrangement.
   h. Notify the archivist if you suspect any errors; don't address errors on your own.
   i. Maintain the sequence of folders within the box.
   j. Maintain the sequence of pages within the folder; pages will stay in order if turned like the pages of a book.
   k. Align folder contents properly as you move through them; don't shake down the contents.

Needless to say, it is very important to enforce policies equally and across the board, regardless of whether the users are internal or external. Some states have directed that local governments in their jurisdiction have very open policies allowing any record that is not part of an active case or investigation to be open for use. Other states may permit records to be closed longer. Also many federal government records can be found at the local level, including documentation of federally funded grant projects and programs. Access is generally open but could be closed for a certain number of years depending on the subject of the grant.

Figure 8.4.  Researchers must leave belongings in assigned lockers to deter theft when they enter most archives. Courtesy City of Portland Archives & Records Center.

An archives should maintain regular, stated hours and should be staffed by someone familiar with the holdings. You need to be sure your researchers are aware of emergency exits and restricted areas, and can provide directional information, such as the location of bathrooms and water fountains. Although it is only a courtesy, a handout or verbal description of local places to eat is often appreciated by out-of-town visitors who may be unfamiliar with your location.

Do not forget that archivists have an ethical responsibility to provide access, but not to provide interpretation. Reference staff should not attempt to interpret legal records for a researcher or provide legal advice, nor should they be expected to explain financial or budget documents. In all cases, staff should be able to explain in general to a researcher what they are looking at, but not make comments or value judgments that would tend to color or influence a researcher. It is up to the researcher to view archival information through his or her own lens.

Access policies should also include details on how copies can be made, whether copies can be made onsite by the researcher, and the cost of copies. Some local archives "charge back" to other government offices for copies, while other archives provide copies to other government offices at no charge. Additional fees may be incurred for photographic prints, oversized copies of maps and plans, and copies of electronic information regardless of format (text, audio, moving image).

Some government records centers charge a research or access fee to people who do not live in the locality. There may be a per-day fee to use the records, which can range widely. Use fees are more commonly charged by private facilities, such as a historical society, which hold government records. Other facilities will charge a nominal fee to answer reference e-mails, letters, and telephone calls. There may be tiered fees, in which one rate is charged to locals and a higher fee for non-taxpayers who live elsewhere.

Finally, it's important to have a plan of action when the requestor speaks another language. Does the archives have bilingual staff who speak common languages such as Spanish or French? Is there ready access to an interpreter in another department who can be brought in, or is it up to the requestor to translate questions? Issues with foreign languages often relate to legal and immigration records.

Access policies are much needed components of providing reference to local government records. The policies should be stated and published. They should be summarized on brochures and be available on websites. The archives should have access to several other vital forms for basic archives operations, including records request forms for use when pulling materials. The archives should also have a reproduction order form. Some archives find it valuable to have preprinted receipts that itemize charges, while others will have simple cash register receipts to offer after payment for copies.

For more information on access policies, see the sample form for access policies and reference services in appendix 2.

## REPROGRAPHY

Most facilities provide access to a photocopier. It is up to the institution to decide whether users may photocopy originals by themselves, or if copying must be done solely by staff. An important part of the reference process is to always examine originals for preservation concerns before allowing any photocopying. The archives should always reserve the right to refuse any technique of reproduction that might endanger the document. A common example is correspondence or letters, which sometimes have creases due to folding. With age creases can become tears, which weaken further and split the item.

Policies vary from place to place, but many archives now permit low-resolution non-professional photography with simple handheld point-and-shoot digital cameras and cell phone cameras. For many researchers and many archivists, the digital camera has become a staple tool for reproductions; they have no effect on the originals, reduce handling and potential damage, reduce staff time, and allow the researcher to leave with reproductions that can be used immediately. The benefits of allowing simple photography often far outweigh any detriments. Your archives will also want to have a listing of other services you might offer, such as price lists for Xerox copies, or digital scanning.

## ACCESS TOOLS

Reference also includes the use of tools to identify and locate collections or records series. Finding aids such as registers, calendars and descriptions, often called inventories or collection guides, help make materials more accessible to researchers. Even a simple printout or database file of collection titles, inclusive dates, and formats will help researchers understand the volume of the materials, subjects, inclusive dates, and general information about the creation and nature of the collection. The finding aid can be as general or as specific as time and labor dictate.

Placing guides and inventories on the archives' website or giving access through online databases improves accessibility to researchers before they ever contact the archives. More detailed finding aids include descriptions of the records and the kinds of materials one might find in the records, a subject catalogue (i.e., for estate records, wills, annual returns, ordinary court minutes, and guardians' letters) and subject guides for specific topics (e.g., descriptions about where to check for local genealogical or Civil War materials). Good finding aids will lessen the researchers' dependence on staff while making the records more open to the public.

A subject guide, another sort of access tool, identifies different collections or records series relating to a specific topic. Two major examples are Civil War or World War II records relating to a local government. Annotations are especially helpful if the subject matter is held within a larger collection that does not appear to relate on the surface. Subject guides are most useful for subjects that are researched frequently. Suggested areas for subject guides might include "researching neighborhoods"; "researching governing bodies and elected officials"; "bond elections"; "transportation"; and "historic public works projects. The key to remember is that collections can be combined or divided on paper but not in actuality. Military records that are part of the Clerk of Courts files can be listed with Civil War Records (for pension documents), World War I and World War II (for draft registration), and Vietnam and later conflicts for lists of local citizens who served.

## DOCUMENTING REFERENCE WORK

An archives should record the number of people using your archives. You may have separate categories for in-house research visits, e-mail queries, and notations about the types of materials used. These numbers will be very important in showing funders, top management, and board members that your archives is important to other people and, more importantly, is being used. Tally sheets can be kept at the reference desk and compiled weekly or monthly into a statistical report. While few people enjoy generating statistical data, it is an important component of the grant application process, since archives are often asked to demonstrate level of use and other information.

Tax-paying citizens deserve to be treated for who they are—the people who fund your local government and ultimately, your archives program. Never forget that public records belong to "The People." Polite and effective reference services help save time and money in locating collections, answer questions in a timely manner, help users to frame their research strategy and expand the scope of research, and prevent materials from improper handling and damage. All of these practices contribute to the larger goal of transparency and accountability in government.

## NOTES

1. Mary Jo Pugh, *Providing Reference Service* (Chicago, Society of American Archivists), 252.

2. ADA Accessibility Guidelines in the Americans with Disabilities Act of 1990—ADA—42 U.S. Code Chapter 126, Sections 4, 8.1, and 8.2; Thomas P. Wilsted, "Reference Area," in *Planning New and Remodeled Archival Facilities* (Chicago: Society of American Archivists, 2007), 29–30.

3. William Maher, *The Management of College and University Archives* (Metuchen, NJ: Society of American Archivists and Scarecrow Press, 1992), 135.

# 9

# Outreach and Exhibits

**D**espite being a vital component of a local government, archives and records programs are often overlooked and not always in the public eye. The stereotypical image of an archives filled with dusty records and tucked away in a basement or an attic, with little relevance to today, comes to mind. Archives staff must lead the charge to publicize the fact that the government has an archives, and that it is valuable to the community, through outreach activities and exhibits. This aspect of the archivist's job can be crucial to the long-term success of the archives itself.

Outreach, as defined by Richard Pearce-Moses in *A Glossary of Archival and Records Terminology*, is "the process of identifying and providing services to constituencies with needs relevant to the repository's mission, especially underserved groups, and tailoring services to meet those needs. Outreach activities may include exhibits, workshops, publications, and educational programs." A key part of the definition is that outreach is a process. Outreach involves more than sending out a press release once or twice a year and is instead the total effort to reach out to the various publics served by the archives, including the local government staff who create the records and the public served by the government. Exhibits, organized displays of archival materials, can create a visual image for the archives. Because there are so many different forms of outreach from simple to elaborate, there is almost no excuse for an archives to not do it.

Successfully executed, outreach and exhibits help archives connect with many more people than would normally come into the facility to use archival holdings. Plus, the efforts may generate new users. Outreach can remind everyone, especially records creators inside government, that some of the records being created every day have value beyond their current usage.

Keeping the archives in front of elected officials and budgetary decision makers through outreach efforts is always desirable. In *Outreach: Innovative Practices for Archives and Special Collections*, author Kate Theimer makes the case that "greater public awareness of archives results in greater potential public support for their work."[1]

Publicity and other outreach efforts can announce the availability of materials to researchers, remind government officials of the value of older records and invite students and local history, genealogy, and academic researchers to use the materials in research. Any information about the archives and its collections needs to be accurate and only promise what is actually available, since not every researcher will find what they want, nor will the desired or expected information always be contained in the records.

Publicity can take many forms. Many newspapers, especially in small towns or neighborhood and community papers in big cities, are often happy to run stories based on historic government records. Finding $330 in crisp, little-used bills dating from a Civil War–era probate case made the front page of one local newspaper more than a century after the original event, while finding a local court record signed by attorney and future president Abraham Lincoln also generated national news.

Other publicity can come from giving radio interviews, conducting local history trivia contests taken from historical documents, or providing local history stories for radio or television personalities to use on their shows or as public service announcements. A series of short spots in newspapers, websites, radio, or television about items of historical interest can add much to heritage celebrations and generate interest in the archives. Similarly, a brochure or book featuring historical photographs from the archives' collections can draw attention and excitement to the archives. Every effort should be made to see that the archives receives visible credit for the historical information used in the news spots. Some archives request a gratis copy of the finished product from the user, which is helpful to refer to when explaining the many ways that archival materials are utilized.

Other forms of publicity include archives websites, social media pages, blogs, informational pamphlets about doing research, and periodic archives newsletters. Websites can be prepared by staff or professionally developed and should include information of interest to the general public in addition to basics like hours and accessibility. Brochures can vary in expense and style, from ones printed on quality paper and professionally designed, to those created through desktop publishing.

The focus of brochures can include general archives information, genealogical resources, local history, or other special topics of interest. Brochures can be printed for free distribution and made available on the Internet for a researcher to read or print out. These are effective and often inexpensive ways to spread the word about the archives. An archives might also sponsor workshops and classes on local history or genealogy to encourage use of local records and give tours to school groups, service organizations, and Scout troops. Presenting programs to local civic clubs can be another effective way to reach other audiences. Every effort should be made to see that copies of the archives' newsletters, brochures, and press releases are available to both the general public and members of the governing body so that they have an idea about what the archives is doing.

Outreach efforts can be timed to keep the archival program's presence regularly before the public and local government's officials/employees. Even between events there is time to keep people informed. If you have examples of previous stories about the archives from newspaper clippings, keep photocopies handy to make up an instant "press kit" that can be shared with media or individuals. Stories culled from old records don't date very quickly and have a fairly long shelf life.

Outreach can easily be done by both "lone arrangers" and staffs of more than one person. Volunteers or assistants can be trained to give presentations and write newspaper and newsletter articles. Publicity, especially in the words of citizens, helps present the image of the archives as a place to gain a better understanding of the past, present, and future of the locality.

A major component of outreach and exhibit activities is to make it a process. Occasional one-shot efforts can sometimes be effective, but having a clear plan ensures a more positive outcome and helps guide future activities at the archives. Knowing your various constituencies and being willing to experiment with different kinds of outreach activities can help guide you. Setting dates for when various tasks should be done, and knowing who should be doing what can make things easier whether you are planning routine press releases or newsletters or planning a new exhibit. Creating reminders about tasks that need to be done or followed up on and calendars can also help save time and energy. Since archives are frequently understaffed, careful planning can help ensure outreach efforts do not get forgotten in the midst of other major projects.

Another key part of planning outreach and exhibits is to scale displays and events to the size of your archives. If you aren't the Smithsonian Institution or a major archives with many staff members devoted just to the event or the exhibit, don't try to do a blockbuster event. Or if you plan a major exhibit and opening, you should know that it will take most of your staff's time and resources. You need to be able to do a program or an exhibit well, and you need to have staff members or volunteers who can help you or vendors you can call upon before you undertake a new project. Conversely, you and your institution need to be willing to experiment and try new activities to maintain and encourage interest from the public and keep things fresh.

## MEDIA RELATIONS

Providing information for newspapers, television, radio, and other entities is an activity that must be handled with care and awareness. If you work for a local government, then you are an agent and representative of that government. Your press releases may be used in full or the releases may lead the press to ask more questions. Always remember when you respond to an email message or a telephone call that "anything you say can and will be used against you." Do not express your private opinions on a government subject or person during work time, as it may paint your government in an unflattering light or worse, you may violate personnel rules regarding speaking to outside media.

When you are contacted by a reporter or writer, how should you behave? To put the archives' best foot forward, it is important to be friendly and un-obstructive. Even if the media representative is aggressive or rude, you must always remember your role as an ambassador of local government. Unless you are already clear on policy, be sure to find out if your higher ups will permit you to speak to media. Depending on what the questions are, you may be able to handle some of them easily, while others may be more convoluted and best answered by a person higher up in the chain of authority.

Remember, in an interview setting you are potentially being recorded or the requestor may be taking notes. If you are not permitted to interact with media, politely refer the person to the proper individual. In government environments, reporters are frequently hungry for information and particularly for fuel for controversy. Be aware that the person calling you may not always be forthcoming about their motivations and intentions.

On the other hand, it is important to help news agencies understand that the archives is there to assist them. When an elected official such as a former mayor, council member, commissioner, or department head dies, the archives is potentially one of the first places news agencies will call for information about their dates in office, pertinent facts about their government career, and most often a photograph. Because grieving families often do not have the time or interest to find an appropriate photo, having ready access to images is vital and supportive to everyone involved.

## FORMS OF OUTREACH

Outreach can be fun for an archivist because it provides a break from the usual routines of accessioning and processing collections and supervising researchers. Outreach utilizes a variety of skills including writing, planning, and graphic design and provides opportunities for staff members to show their creative sides. Outreach itself can take many forms: press releases, newsletters, brochures, e-mail blasts, social media, and special events such as lectures, commemorations, and symposia. Even online digital libraries and collaborative projects such as the Portal to Texas History or the Digital Library of Georgia, where individual institutions share historical records, can be considered a type of outreach.

The fact that outreach comes in many different forms presents a challenge in itself: you can spend so much time reaching out to new constituents that you do not have time to handle the responsibilities in your archives. This is especially true in small archives with only one or two staff members. Various aspects of outreach take time. You need an interesting topic to be presenting to the press or on social media. Press releases need to be informative and well written. Unless you have computer skills to handle the e-mail blasts or the social media posts or have the artistic skills to create the program for a symposium, don't be shy about getting help. Graphic design can be time consuming, especially when you do not do it all the time.

Similarly, brochures, websites, and email blasts need to look good *and* have engaging and well-written content to effectively reach the public. If you don't have an internal public information office or communications director, communications and public history students from a nearby college or university can assist with generating ideas, doing research, and handling social media or graphic design. You may be able to get these students to volunteer with your archives or do an internship with you.

Volunteers with journalism or marketing skills can be a major coup to an archives if you are lucky enough to find one. The biggest challenge is to decide what you want to do, be willing to experiment, and to try to do what you do well. Be realistic about what you can and cannot do. Do what you have time to do well and appreciate the fact that, with few exceptions, you cannot do everything.

## DEVELOPING EXHIBITS

Exhibits are a traditional form of outreach and can be assembled by staff at most archives. Exhibits can be fairly simple, such as a few key photographs or documents focusing on one topic with brief captions. Or they can be a larger and more involved look at a major topic. Exhibits can increase public visibility and serve as subtle but constant reminders that the government has an archives which is helping to preserve its history. Exhibits can also be adapted according to the anticipated audience and the particular display area.

Exhibits in local governments can be mounted in any number of environments: in government building hallways with consistent citizen foot traffic; in areas where citizens spend time waiting or standing around (licensing and fine-paying areas are especially valued); or even inside the archives researcher area. They can consist of wall-mounted cases or floor cases which can be moved around as needed. Or if enclosures are not feasible, reproductions of photographs and documents mounted on foam core board can make simple, effective exhibits nearly anywhere.

Exhibit areas within archives researcher areas are prized for displaying original items because they are not only under constant supervision, but also because they provide something to look at while waiting. In other areas with less supervision, originals are acceptable for display if they are in secure cabinetry and not subjected to environmental extremes such as excessive light, heat, or cold.

Inside the archives, exhibit themes themselves can be broad. For instance, a theme about treasures found in the archives allows you to spotlight a variety of records, including the oldest, newest, most significant, and most popular items identified by archivists or used by researchers. Such an exhibit could feature the city charter; photographs from a visit by a president, governor, or other official; film footage from a natural disaster that impacted your area; and historic election records. Choose a few select items and keep captions and explanatory material brief. In exhibits, less is more.

Exhibits located outside the archives can have an even greater impact on the public visibility of your institution but also come with security concerns. The local government may already have display cases which you can use periodically. You may also be able to work with other offices to develop exhibits. Your archives may be eligible for grants from a local or state nonprofit or through state programs to purchase display cases so that you can have temporary exhibits that you change out every few months.

Another option might be to create reproduction photographs (with or without frames) and mount them in visible, well-traveled hallways. Themes for these displays can vary greatly: historic broadsides and flyers and images relating to the local economy; maps over several decades; or excerpts from important documents of the government. You could also do more traditional displays of portraits of council members, commissioners, or police chiefs or sheriffs along with brief biographies. Such photos can be livened up with occasional shots of police cars or government buildings from earlier years.

## TYPES OF EXHIBITS

Exhibits can be simple or elaborate. One exhibit might be housed in just one or two display cases while another spreads across several rooms in a

Figure 9.1a.    An exhibit case near the entrance of a local government archives features rotating exhibits. Displays engage and connect the public to history and educate citizens about the archives' holdings. Courtesy City of Portland Archives & Records Center.

gallery. Exhibits can also be online on a portion of the archives' website or be a more extensive affair with interactive elements. Regardless of size, exhibits in government archives usually fall into three basic types: historical, interpretive, and informational. Informational exhibits are often simple and oriented around a particular theme. Perhaps your government has opened a new or renovated building. This is a great opportunity to spotlight architects' drawings, historic photos of construction, and publicity about the structure. Captions can be brief or may not be needed at all. A historical component can include older maps or pre-construction photographs—the building before preservation took place or the site in earlier years.

Another type of informational exhibit can focus on what the archives does and how staff preserve materials. These exhibits are a great way to share basic details about the day-to-day work of archivists. They can be an especially nice way to conclude a major project. For an actual or online exhibit about a major grant to arrange and scan early documents of the government, you could create an informational display featuring photos of volunteers working with documents, along with enlarged photographs of scanned images. You could use temporary desktop board displays that get changed out every few weeks and sit on a table near the research area. You can provide giveaways like bookmarks or pencils featuring the web address.

Historical exhibits for local government archives, needless to say, are popular because you can use a variety of types of documents and photographs in one exhibit. An exhibit about the history of a government department or a major government construction project might feature photographs of the department through the years, copies of pages from original minute books about the construction, and engineering maps and plans. Historical exhibits may need lengthier captions to explain what the different items are and how they relate to the exhibit subject and to each other. Archives are especially well poised to participate in major government anniversaries.

Interpretative exhibits can be similar to other sorts of exhibits, but generally require more explanation from the exhibit's curator or the archivist. Concise captions are a crucial part of the exhibit and include text explaining the meaning of each item in the display. In the words of Jessica Lacher-Feldman, interpretive labels "introduce information about the materials being exhibited and allow the exhibit designers to share their own ideas and explain why specific items were chosen. This allows the exhibit designers to add value to the collections by explaining their historical, cultural, or symbolic significance and placing them in a broader context."[2]

Interpretive exhibits offer a chance for archivists who have been working with the collections for lengthy periods to explain to people what they are looking at and the importance of items. In the case of a public works project—like the construction of a major bridge or a roadway—an exhibit allows the archivist to add more details to the story—such as the enthusiasm when it was built, comments on social changes (did it unite or divide the community?) along with problems that might have led to its creation or its demise. ·

## PHYSICAL ISSUES OF EXHIBITS

Because archival materials are mostly two-dimensional, displays need to have a strong visual impact and need to look professional. Poorly executed exhibits reflect badly on the archives. Staff may be able to prepare the exhibits or you may need outside help. Preparing exhibits can be a pleasant break in routine for archivists if they have adequate time to focus on the project. Use staff talents and creativity in preparing exhibits. If you supervise archivists, assigning them to work on exhibits can help instill pride in their work. They

**Figure 9.1b.**   Local government archives can play a valuable role in important anniversaries and observances. In 2013 the Dallas Municipal Archives contributed a special exhibit to mark the 50th year since President John F. Kennedy's murder in Dallas in 1963. Courtesy Dallas Municipal Archives, City of Dallas, Texas.

are usually delighted when items in the collections are seen and appreciated by the public.

To learn more about developing and mounting exhibits, state and regional associations of archives or museum professionals often hold workshops about creating exhibits; there is also plenty of information on the Internet about developing effective displays. One good way to learn about exhibits is simply to look at examples in other archives and museums. Are there ideas or topics that you can easily adopt?

If you are in an area with colleges or universities, look for people who might assist you. Students, especially those in public history and museum studies classes, might help. Reach out to faculty and museum professionals if possible and explain what you need; students may be able to claim

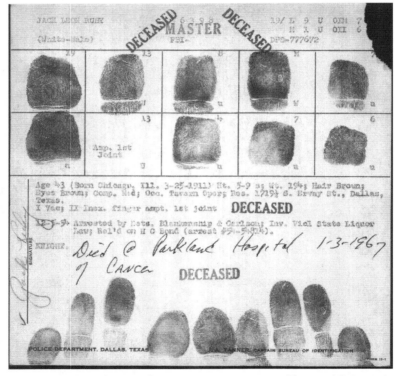

**Figure 9.1c. Rarely seen documents can generate widespread interest in archival materials. In 2013 the Dallas Municipal Archives displayed assassin Jack Ruby's fingerprint card in an exhibit marking the 50th year since President John F. Kennedy's murder in Dallas in 1963. Courtesy Dallas Municipal Archives, City of Dallas, Texas.**

course credit in return for design and fabrication work. A last avenue to be explored is to hire exhibit design professionals. This can be a good option if you have funds, especially if the exhibits are long-term or semi-permanent exhibits.

## EXHIBIT OPENINGS AND EVENTS

Exhibit openings and special events offer another chance to connect with the public. Depending on the size of the exhibit, you might want to have an opening reception or an open house. If your archives is in the same building as your government's governing body, you might hold your event to coincide with their meeting day and break times. Light refreshments are plenty—you don't need to feed people substantially. Other options are to have an exhibit opening during lunch time or an early morning coffee. Regardless of the time of day, the opening gives you a chance to promote your archives to people who might not regularly visit your place, including records creators, citizens, and special guests.

**Figure 9.2.** Archives sometimes host special events such as a ribbon-cutting cermony for the new vault at the Dallas Municipal Archives. The event was open to the public and was attended by Mayor Mike Rawlings and former Mayor Wes Wise, as well as members of the Dallas City Council. Courtesy Dallas Morning News.

Figure 9.3.  Public events draw the public as well as elected officials into archives and highlight the importance of the documents. Courtesy Harris County Archives, Houston, TX.

You will need to create some kind of invitation to the event. It could be an e-mail invitation also posted on social media, or you might have nice invitations or postcards printed at a relatively modest cost if the event is more than casual. Don't forget to invite archives volunteers or students. If you are able to offer giveaways such as pencils or printed bookmarks, attendees will have something to remind them of the archives.

## LOGISTICS OF EXHIBITS

Because you may be using original documents and photographs, there are several areas of concern with exhibits which you do not have with other forms of outreach.

### Security

Security is a major issue. You don't want to run the risk that an original item can easily be stolen or damaged. Any kind of original document is at risk of being stolen if put in an unprotected area. Using locked cases in well-lit areas will often offer ample protection. Depending on where your exhibit is located, high-quality reproductions may be acceptable in lieu of originals. It is now possible to make reproductions that look much like the original, especially when viewed from several feet away. Similarly, enlarged prints of small photos often work much better than the original for an exhibit. A copy would not need to be kept under lock and key.

### Lighting

Lighting is another concern. Be sure that lighting is bright enough to be able to adequately view the item but not so bright as to cause fading of original paper or artifacts. You may want to invest in a light meter to determine whether lights are appropriate for your display area. Guidelines and acceptable light levels for displaying archival documents are detailed in the paper "Guidelines On Exhibiting Archival Materials," prepared by the International Council on Archives.[3]

You might be able to switch to a lower wattage or to a different kind of bulb. Avoid fluorescent light wherever possible. LED (light-emitting diodes) bulbs are becoming more widely available and more affordable. These bulbs put out less heat and last much longer than incandescent, halogen, or fluorescent bulbs. What is most significant about LED lighting is that it does not emit ultraviolet light, the type considered most harmful to paper and photographs.

## Documentation

Proper documentation of materials being used in the exhibit and making sure exhibit items are returned to their proper location once the exhibit is closed is another area where archivists need to take extra precautions. A marker indicating "removed for exhibit," sometimes called an out-card or a separation page, should be used to mark where and when an item has been removed. If possible, a photocopy or photograph of the item removed should be placed with the separation sheets or kept in a database. Additionally, a copy of the separation sheet needs to be kept with the pulled items to facilitate return.

## Environment

Items on display deserve the same environmental care you would show for items in storage. When original items are on display, temperature and humidity settings need to be maintained between 65 and 75 degrees Fahrenheit with stable relative humidity if possible.[4] If you live in a humid climate, unchecked relative humidity can warp paper documents. When in doubt, use a reproduction. You don't want to display the first volume the county ever created near an outside door that is opened and closed many times a day with continual fluctuations in temperature.

Bound volumes need to have "cradle" supports to protect the bindings. Clear Mylar sleeves or thin bands of Mylar can be used to hold a book open to particular pages without forcing the paper. If any of your original materials touch acidic foam core or colored paper in the exhibit case, use acid-free paper to create a barrier between the original and acidic paper; better yet, use acid-free foam core and paper if you are displaying original materials for extended lengths of time.

## Installation and Takedown

Installing and taking down an exhibit that uses original materials from the archives needs to be done with great care. Because you are concentrating on the exhibit surroundings, it's easy to forget about the fragile nature of some archives materials. This is also a time to be extra careful since cases have to be unlocked to remove items. If cases have to be left unattended, then you should lock them before you leave.

## ONLINE EXHIBITS AND SOCIAL MEDIA

Web-based exhibits and blogs are another relatively easy way for archivists to reach out to the public. Like other forms of outreach, they can be as simple or complex as your time and experience allows. Creating online exhibits requires web building and web publishing expertise and requires access to software programs. Some basic programs are often available as freeware and even include simple exhibit templates.

Much like actual exhibits, virtual displays for local government archives can cover a wide variety of topics. They can be scanned versions of actual exhibits or they can be wholly unique and created from scratch. Before mounting online exhibits, you might want to spend time exploring other online exhibits as examples.

Exhibits can be simple static photographs of local government or early legislative documents creating your county, city, or governmental authority. Because the World Wide Web is visually oriented, photographs, maps, and other graphic materials are especially suitable for online viewing. Whether you build the exhibit yourself or use outside help, be sure the files are properly sized for best viewing. Guidelines for image and text sizes are readily available on the Web and in books.

If you are already going to the trouble of creating an online exhibit, why not develop it into an educational tool? With a little more effort, you can perhaps partner with a local historical society, college, or public library; you could create an online history of the area or the government that you could add to periodically. Exhibits with clearly stated facts can be used in local elementary and high schools as teaching tools; schools are particularly grateful if lesson plans are included. Teachers, graduate students, and others are sometimes available to help craft a lesson plan.

Blogging, the web-based equivalent of a journal, is a somewhat more interactive way to disseminate information about the archives. In blog entries, the archives can highlight a single item and tell its story, or describe an entire collection. Blog programs and templates are easy to find and usually free or very inexpensive. Most blogs are interactive, allowing visitors to leave comments. It is this interactivity that goes beyond static web exhibits, encouraging social relations between readers and other bloggers. In more than a few instances, comments left on blogs have helped identify previously unknown people, places, and events in photographs.

Promoting archives through virtual communities such as Facebook and tweeting is immediate and surprising in its ability to reach consumers of social media. While they are like blogs, they operate even faster and the nearly instantaneous exchange of comments and information can generate intense interest in a collection or an item from the archives.

The most appealing aspects of online exhibits and social media use are that you can have an attractive, meaningful presence at simple or elaborate levels, but also an immediateness that helps create an experience of archives and archival collections that is personal and meaningful.

## BEYOND OUTREACH AND EXHIBITS: PUBLIC PROGRAMS

Once your local government archives has become established and you are able to think beyond day-to-day operations, you may want to start thinking about special events. By this point, you should have an ongoing outreach program and you periodically send press releases out and regularly communicate with supporters through printed newsletters or e-mail and social media updates. It may be time to host public programs or workshops and prepare special publications. You might publish an exhibit catalog or host a conference on a topic of importance to local and regional history.

Before launching public programs and special publications, you should carefully review the outreach plan and long-range goals of your institutions. While the new programs may be different from other activities of your archives, they should support your general goals and promote your archives and its activities.

Lectures by noted historians, professors, public and amateur historians who are experienced speakers, and archives researchers or experts in topics related to the archives are traditional public programs that many archives hold on a regular basis. Talks are sometimes linked to brown-bag or ticketed lunches or dinners. Most governments have guidelines to follow regarding fund-raising.

Before holding a public event, consider the logistics—does your facility have space? Will it be a free event open to the public, or do you expect to charge admission? Do you want to make money or break even? This will help you decide about pricing, should you opt for a fund-raiser. Will you serve food or light refreshments? What kind of publicity do you need to do?

For larger events, you might consider a conference that will feature multiple speakers and will last for a morning or afternoon, or perhaps a full day. This might be an especially popular happening if your archives is located near a college or university. Be sure you have in mind who the targeted audience is, and how to get the word out. You might also consider whether you will want to publish a volume of the proceedings of the conference, which might be sold later or made available as an online publication that readers can download. Simple photocopied program notes are also an inexpensive option.

Special exhibits sometimes warrant exhibit catalogs. Catalogs and publications are especially appealing when issued in conjunction with commemorations of events that have significance beyond the locality, such as the fiftieth anniversary of the assassination of President John F. Kennedy or the March on Selma and the voting rights movement. In both cases, local government archives marked the observances with exhibits and publications.

Another kind of publication that can help promote a major event is a pictorial history. These books can be time-consuming projects, but can be relatively inexpensive to the organization to publish. Some commercial publishers have contracts where the local organization does not have to put money up in advance of publication. The author or the institution will have to follow the company's guidelines and may be able to secure royalties or a percentage of the sales of the books. The options are fairly endless and such publications can certainly promote the work of the archives.

Another opportunity for public programming can occur during American Archives Month, which is annually observed each October. In solidarity with the archives profession, archivists are encouraged to join colleagues from across the country in declaring October to be American Archives Month. This observance is a collaborative effort by professional organizations and repositories around the nation to highlight the importance of records of enduring value. By recognizing Archives Month, your local government is highlighting the valuable work done by archivists and the value of archives in daily life. It is a time to focus on the importance of records of enduring value and to enhance public recognition for the people and programs that are responsible for maintaining our communities' vital historical records. Sample proclamations and ample information on advocacy are available through the Society of American Archivists.

Outreach and exhibit programs offer almost limitless possibilities to local government archives to engage and attract the public. The only limitations are time, funding, and the creativity of staff and volunteers, and how the activity will promote the mission of the archives.

## NOTES

1. Kate Theimer, "More about Outreach: Innovative Practices for Archives and Special Collections" (ArchivesNext). http://www.archivesnext.com/?p=3806.

2. Jessica Lacher-Feldman, *Exhibits in Archives and Special Collections Libraries* (Chicago: Society of American Archivists, 2013), 66.

3. Yola de Lusenet, Simon Lunn, and Anna Michaś, eds., *Guidelines on Exhibiting Archival Materials* (Paris: International Council on Archives Committee on Preservation of Archives in Temperate Climates, 2006), 43–47.

4. Lacher-Feldman, *Exhibits in Archives*, 56.

# Appendix 1

## Sample Legislative Document to Establish an Archives

AN ORDINANCE relating to the City of Seattle archives and records management activities; combining the duties and responsibilities for archives and records management in one division of the Office of the City Clerk; creating a Seattle Archives and Records Management Program; amending Seattle Municipal Code (SMC) Chapter 3.122; repealing SMC Chapter 3.123; amending SMC Chapter 3.42.040; repealing SMC Chapter 3.42.050; and amending SMC Chapter 3.125.

WHEREAS, Ordinance 111782 established the Seattle Municipal Archives program in the Office of the City Clerk, and Ordinance 120736 established the City Records Management Program in the Office of the City Clerk; and

WHEREAS, merging the Seattle Municipal Archives and the City Records Management Program will result in greater efficiency and coordination in the management of records and archives through their entire life cycle; and

WHEREAS, records are required for government to carry out business activities, to document actions and decisions and to maintain continuity in governance; and

WHEREAS, all records created in city government are public records, and it is necessary to provide a comprehensive system of integrated procedures for the management of records, for efficient, economical and effective controls over the creation, distribution, organization, maintenance, use and disposition of all City of Seattle public records in accordance with State laws and regulations; and

WHEREAS, certain records retain long term business and/or archival value and must be preserved to sustain enterprise functions, support accountability, and provide historical information and evidence of City activity; and

WHEREAS, the City is planning the creation of an Electronic Records Management Initiative to comprehensively manage the digital records created and received by City agencies; and

WHEREAS, the City Council and the Mayor recognize the value and vital business necessity of a Citywide Archives and Records Management Program; NOW, THEREFORE,

**BE IT ORDAINED BY THE CITY OF SEATTLE AS FOLLOWS:**

**Section 1. Chapter 3.122 of the Seattle Municipal Code, which chapter was last amended by Ordinance 111782, is amended as follows:**

**Chapter 3.122 Seattle Archives and Records Management Program**

**3.122.010 City of Seattle Archives and Records Management Program established.**

There shall be established a City of Seattle Archives and Records Management Program in the Office of the City Clerk. The purpose of the Seattle Archives and Records Management Program is to provide for efficient, economical and effective controls over public records created by the City throughout their lifecycle. The authority and duties enumerated in this Chapter will apply to all City agencies and all City records will be maintained, disposed of, or preserved in accordance with this program.

**3.122.020 Definitions**

For the purposes of this Chapter, the following definitions apply unless the context otherwise requires:

A. "Agency" means all City departments, divisions, offices, commissions, boards, committees, public corporations (development authorities) or other organizational units created by the City Charter, the Council of the City of Seattle or the Executive Branch of the City of Seattle.

B. "Archival value" means the ongoing usefulness or significance of records, based on the administrative, legal, fiscal, evidential, or historical information they contain, justifying their continued preservation.

C. "Archival Records" means the records created or received by a City agency in the conduct of business and preserved because of the archival value of the information they contain or the evidence of the functions and responsibilities of their creator.

D. "Archives" means the Seattle Municipal Archives, which is the program responsible for maintaining the City's archival records.

E. "Published documents" means reports, studies, or other information, regardless of format, and intended for wide distribution to city government or the public, including documents published by city agencies; reports by consultants hired by the City; and publications of joint projects supported by Seattle City government. Examples of published documents may include annual, biennial, and special reports required by law, city agency newsletters, periodicals, and magazines, and other informational material intended for general dissemination to city agencies or the public.

F. "Record" or "City record" or "Public record" means any information, regardless of physical form or characteristic, prepared, owned, used, received or retained in connection with the transaction of official City business and preserved or appropriate for preservation by an agency as evidence of the organization, function, policies, decisions, procedures, operations or other activities of the City of Seattle, or appropriate for preservation because of the informational value it contains.

### 3.122.030 Seattle Archives and Records Management Program Administration.

There shall be a director of the Seattle Archives and Records Management Program who will have general administrative responsibility for development and implementation of the program. The director shall have authority to establish City-wide policies and rules related to the management of records. Such rules shall be established pursuant to the requirements of the Administrative Code (Ordinance 10228) as now or hereafter amended. The director shall be either the City Archivist or the City Records Manager and will be appointed by the City Clerk.

A. There shall be a City Archivist who is responsible for the operation of the Seattle Municipal Archives, and the care and custody of archival records. The City Archivist will supervise the Archives staff and develop and recommend policies and procedures related to archival records.

B. There shall be a City Records Manager who is responsible for the operation of the City Records Management Program. The City Records Manager will supervise the records management staff and develop and recommend policies and procedures related to the management of current and non-current records.

**3.122.040 Scope of the Seattle Archives and Records Management Program.**

The scope of the Seattle Archives and Records Management Program may include, but is not limited to:

A. Operate the program and the Archives facilities in accordance with currently accepted archives and records management professional standards;

B. Acquire, receive, appraise and secure records of archival value from agencies of the City of Seattle when those records are no longer necessary for conducting current business;

C. Acquire, receive, appraise, and secure all records for areas annexed by the City from a county or special district or from a defunct agency of the City of Seattle;

D. Negotiate for the acquisition and return of City records which have been removed from its possession;

E. Secure transfer of records to the Archives when it has been determined that the records are stored under conditions that do not meet the standards established by Archives and Records Management;

F. Maintain inventories, indexes, catalogs, and other finding aids or guides to facilitate access to the Municipal Archives;

G. Analyze, develop and provide written standards and procedures for the care and maintenance of City records, including those created and/or maintained in electronic format;

H. Establish recordkeeping requirements for business systems or applications that maintain official City records;

I. Provide access, as defined by State law and City policies, to the records within Archives and Records Management's custodianship;

J. Establish procedures for City agencies regarding the identification, segregation, and protection of records vital and essential to continuing operations to comply with the City's emergency preparedness policies;

K. Establish standards for City agencies with regard to the appropriate use of record media, accounting for cost, access and preservation;

L. Establish procedures for the preparation of records inventories and descriptions, and develop records retention schedules which meet the requirements of Washington State Secretary of State's office;

M. Exercise final authority regarding the disposal of City Records and establish procedures for the prompt and orderly disposition of City records which no longer possess administrative, legal, or research value to warrant their retention;

N. Provide a complete curriculum of records management and archives training sessions to all City agencies and employees in order to assist them in meeting their business needs for managing records;
> 1. Coordinate with the Personnel Director in development and maintenance of records management curriculum to be included in new employee orientation, and update curriculum as needed;
> 2. Coordinate with the Personnel Director in establishment and maintenance of a personnel rule to ensure records management training of appropriate current City employees, and update rule as needed;

O. Provide records management advice and assistance to all City agencies and employees as needed for special projects or to allow for the effective management of their records.

P. Administer the Digital Image Management Program as defined and described in SMC chapter 3.125.

**3.122.050 Responsibilities of Elected Officials and Agency Directors/ Managers in regards to Archives and Records Management.**

Records are vital to an open and transparent government process; therefore each City elected official and agency director/manager shall:

A. Adopt and implement policies regarding the creation and preservation of records containing adequate documentation of the organization, functions, policies, decisions, procedures and essential transactions of the agency which are designed to furnish the information necessary to protect the legal and financial rights of the City and of persons directly affected by the agency's activities;

B. Ensure that staff are provided with adequate training and resources to comply with City records policies and procedures established by Archives and Records Management;

C. Work cooperatively with Archives and Records Management to develop and review records retention schedules for records maintained by the agency;

D. Inform Archives and Records Management of any regulatory changes affecting record retention, maintenance or access requirements;

E. Notify Archives and Records Management of any program changes that may affect the management of City records, including but not limited to, new agency responsibilities; records that are no longer being created; and changes to records maintenance practices;

F. Follow established procedures to identify, segregate and protect records vital to the continuing operation of an agency in the event of natural or man-made disaster;

G. Ensure that at least one copy of each published document, as defined in section 3.122.020E, prepared for the City, on behalf of the City or in conjunction with the City, be deposited with the Archives;

H. Notify Archives and Records Management of record categories in the agency's possession that have passed their legal retention, and transfer control of original archival records upon notification from Archives and Records Management;

I. Establish safeguards against unauthorized or unlawful removal, loss or destruction of City records and establish procedures for the review of records when an employee departs the City to ensure that all City Records have been retained appropriately;

J. Adopt and implement policies and procedures to ensure that City records in agency custody are maintained in an manner that meets guidelines set by Archives and Records Management for ensuring security, preservation, legibility, and accessibility;

K. Designate a management level employee as Records Coordinator to act as a liaison between the agency and Archives and Records Management on all matters relating to the Archives and Records Management program.

### 3.122.060 Care of Records.

Records of the City of Seattle shall be managed according to the controlling provisions of the Revised Code of Washington, Washington Administrative Code and this Chapter.

### 3.122.070 Use of Copies.

A City employee performing duties under this Chapter in order to comply with Archives and Records Management guidelines is authorized to copy records in any manner which produces a permanent, clear, accurate and durable reproduction of the original record. An original City record which is worn or damaged may be replaced by a reproduction made in accordance with Archives and Records Management guidelines. Certification by the City Clerk, City Attorney, Archives and Records Management Program, or by the agency having custody of the record that the replacement is a true and correct copy of the original shall accompany the reproduction. When original City records are reproduced and placed in conveniently accessible files, and provisions are made for preserving and using them for the duration of their legally mandated retention, the originals from which they were made may be destroyed.

### 3.122.080 Public Access to Records.

Upon request, all City records, except for those exempted or prohibited from disclosure by applicable law, shall be available for inspection and copying by the public according to procedures that prevent excessive interference with other essential functions of the Agency. Any Agency may require that review of records occurs pursuant to an appointment during certain business hours and at specified locations, and may charge fees to recover actual copying costs for providing copies of public records.

# Appendix 2

## Sample Forms for Local Government Archives

The forms included in this appendix are copyright free and were adapted from forms in use in local government archives. Users are encouraged to adapt these forms to the needs of their particular local government.

# RECORDS INVENTORY

(1) RECORDS OF: _____
          (OFFICE / DEPARTMENT)                  (UNIT)

(2) RECORDS SERIES TITLE: _____

(3) LOCATION OF RECORDS: _____

(4) DESCRIPTION: _____
_____

(5) DATES: From : _____   To: _____

| (6) Are records still created? (Circle answer) answers):<br>  Yes      No<br>(7) Are these Vital Records?  Yes   No | (8) Quantity / Volume: | (9) Arrangement (Circle<br><br>Alphabetical      Numerical<br>Chronological    Subject |
|---|---|---|
| (10) Record media / format (Circle answers)<br>Paper     Bound Volumes     Mylar<br><br>Microform:  16mm   35mm  Microfiche<br><br>Electronic Record: Tape  Reel  Cassette<br>         Diskette  CD-ROM  Optical Disk | | (11) Reference to records (Circle answers):<br><br>Daily / Weekly / Monthly / Yearly for _____<br><br>Never after  _____ |
| 12) Recommended retention period for each type of record: | | (13) Schedule No. Assigned:<br><br><br>(14) Inventory taken by: _____ |

Explanation of form parts:

(1) Write in the name of the office, division, or unit to which the records belong.
(2) Write in the title of the records series. Use a separate form for each records series at each location.
(3) Give the exact location of the records. Be sure to include all storage areas.
(4) Provide a brief description of the records series, including form numbers when applicable.
(5) Indicate the beginning and ending dates of the records series, e.g., May 1956 to April 1965.
(6) Circle if the records are still created.
(7) Circle if the records are considered "Vital" for your office to function daily.
(8) Indicate the volume or quantity of the records. It may be in cubic feet, number of volumes / microfiche, rolls of microfilm, or reels of computer tape. This will help you plan your storage needs. A cubic foot is 12"x12"x12" or 1728 cubic inches.
(9) Circle how the records are arranged, i.e. in numerical order, chronological order, alphabetical order, subject file etc.
(10) Circle whether the record is created and stored on paper, microfilm, computer tape, etc. Circle ALL formats your office uses for this record. Remember to schedule and assign a schedule number to each type of media.
(11) Indicate how often the records are used. For example: daily for 1 year; never after 3 years.
(12) Write in a recommended retention period.
(13) Assign a unique schedule number for this records series which will clearly identify it on all paperwork in the future. If the records are included on an existing approved schedule, write in the schedule number for reference.
(14) Sign and date the form.
Additional Remarks or Notations for your use:

# Archives Regulations for Use

The Archives is a repository of records that facilitates research and documents the activities and history of local government. The Archives is open to anyone agreeing to abide by its regulations for the use of materials. Citizens are required to provide a driver's license number on the reverse of this sheet. The following regulations are intended to help preserve the Archive's historically and permanently valuable materials for future generations.

1. Briefcases, notebooks, binders, notepads, bags, purses, and other personal property are not permitted in the proximity of archives materials. These items will be secured during your visit.

2. Researchers may take only loose sheets of notepaper or notecards into the research area. Sheets of paper are available from the archivist. Materials taken from the research area may be checked prior to the researcher's departure.

3. Pencils only may be used in the proximity of archival materials. Ink pens of any kind are prohibited. Personal computers may be used. If you need a power source, please consult the archivist.

4. Archives materials must be handled with great care, as follows:

   a. Make no marks, erasures, or any other changes to the documents.

   b. Keep all items on the table while being used. Place nothing in the lap or propped against the table.

   c. Place nothing on top of archives materials; do not write on top of, alter, lean on, fold anew, or trace materials.

   d. Turn pages slowly and carefully, touching only the margins if possible.

   e. Wear the gloves provided when working with photographic materials.

   f. Remove materials from boxes and open folders to use documents or to insert photoduplication sheets.

   g. Keep collections in their existing order and arrangement.

   h. Notify the archivist if you suspect any errors; don't address errors on your own.

   i. Maintain the sequence of folders within the box.

   j. Maintain the sequence of pages within the folder; pages will stay in order if turned like the pages of a book.

   k. Align folder contents properly as you move through them; don't shake down the contents.

I have read and agree to abide by the Regulations for Use.

Name _____

Date _____

Address _____ Driver's License Number/State
_____

# CITY/COUNTY ARCHIVES
## PHOTOGRAPHIC REPRODUCTION SERVICES

| Price List | |
|---|---|
| **Standard paper photocopy** Each side that has recorded Information is considered a page. | |
| | |
| **Reproduction Fee** | |
| Digital reproduction for a onetime publication or website use in a single language in one country. This fee does not include charges for broadcast or publishing copyright permission. | |
| | |
| **Preservation Fee** For-profit broadcast or publishing permission, per image: | |
| Commercial exhibition | |
| Commercial reproduction or resale | |
| Onetime print use in a single language, worldwide | |
| Onetime print or electronic (e-book) use in all languages, worldwide. | |
| One-country broadcast use in a single language only | |
| World broadcast use in a single language only | |
| World broadcast use in all languages | |
| | |
| **Nonprofit Fee** For nonprofit broadcast or publishing permission, per image: | |
| Commercial exhibition | |
| Commercial reproduction or resale | |
| Onetime print use in a single language worldwide | |
| Onetime print or electronic (e-book) use in all languages worldwide | |
| One-country broadcast use in a single language only | |

### Notice Regarding Copyright and Ownership

The Archives charges nonprofit and commercial preservation fees in order to support the maintenance of our collections. Possessing reproductions of the Archives' materials does not constitute permission to use. While the majority of materials in the Archives are public records, the government asserts its ownership of the originals. Materials owned by the Archives are not considered Public Domain. When using our images for publication, display, or broadcast, please cite the source as "Courtesy City/County Archives."

### Digital Scanning & FTP Delivery

Images can be scanned at up to 1200 dpi and produced from transparencies, negatives, or prints up to 8x10. In most cases the Archives can provide a File Transfer Protocol site [FTP] from which images can be downloaded. After payment the address is sent to you and the images will remain at that site for 72 hours before the link is removed. Upon request files can be transferred to portable drive compact disk in most standard file formats. Images are for onetime use only and may not be used for future publication or broadcast without additional authorization or payment of fees.

**Processing Time**

Turnaround time for photographic reproductions is seven to fourteen working days (no service on weekends or holidays) though can be longer due to backlogged orders. Turnaround time is approximate from the date of receipt. **The Archives is unable to accept rush orders and users are urged to plan accordingly.**

**Billing and Handling**

All orders must be prepaid. Domestic mail orders will be sent first class. Orders may also be sent via overnight mail services if charged to requestor's account.

**Credit Line**

The required citation for Archives materials used with permission in a publication, display, or any presentation should read as follows:

[Collection Title]
Courtesy The Archives

**The Archives requires a complimentary copy of any product reproducing Archives images.**

# Bibliography

Association for Library Collections and Technical Services (ALCTS). "Guidelines for Preservation Photocopying of Replacement Pages" (1990). Accessed September 22, 2015. http://www.ala.org/alcts/resources/preserv/presvphotocop.

Avery, Cheryl, and Mona Holmlund, eds. *Better Off Forgetting? Essays on Archives, Public Policy, and Collective Memory*. Toronto: University of Toronto Press, 2010.

Boles, Frank. *Selecting and Appraising Archives and Manuscripts*. Archival Fundamentals Series II. Chicago: Society of American Archivists, 2005.

Carmicheal, David W. *Organizing Archival Records: A Practical Method of Arrangement and Description for Small Archives*. Walnut Grove, CA: Alta Mira Press, 2012.

Dallas City Code of Civil and Criminal Ordinances. Chapter 39c—Records Management Program. Accessed July 14, 2014. http://www.amlegal.com/nxt/gateway.dll/Texas/dallas/volumei/preface?f=templates$fn=default.htm$3.0$vid=amlegal:dallas_tx.

de Lusenet, Yola, Simon Lunn, and Anna Michaś, eds., *Guidelines on Exhibiting Archival Materials*. Paris: International Council on Archives, Committee on Preservation of Archives in Temperate Climates, 2007.

Dearstyne, Bruce W., *The Management of Local Government Records: A Guide for Local Government Officials.* Nashville, TN: American Association of State and Local History, 1988.

Finch, Elsie Freeman, ed. *Advocating Archives: An Introduction to Public Relations for Archivists*. Lanham, MD: Society of American Archivists and Scarecrow Press, 2003.

Greene, Mark, and Dennis Meissner, "More Product, Less Process: Revamping Traditional Archival Processing." *American Archivist* 68, no. 2 (Fall/Winter 2005): 212–13.

Holmes, Oliver Wendell. "Archival Arrangement—Five Different Operations at Five Different Levels." *American Archivist* 27 no. 1 (January 1964): 21–41.

Jones, Norvell M. M. "Archival Copies of Thermofax, Verifax, and Other Unstable Records." National Archives Technical Information paper Number 5 American Library Association and Association for Library Collections and Technical Services, 1990.

Kite, Marion, and Roy Thomson, eds., *Conservation of Leather: and Related Materials.* Oxford: Elsevier Butterworth-Heinemann, 2006.

Lacher-Feldman, Jessica. *Exhibits in Archives and Special Collections Libraries.* Chicago: Society of American Archivists, 2013.

Lowell, Waverly, and Nelb, Tawny Ryan, *Architectural Records: Managing Design and Construction Records.* Chicago: Society of American Archivists, 2006.

Maher, William. *The Management of College and University Archives.* Metuchen, NJ: Society of American Archivists and Scarecrow Press, 1992.

Mattern, Ellen. *The Replevin Process in Government Archives: Recovery and the Contentious Question of Ownership.* Doctoral dissertation, University of Pittsburgh, 2014.

Miller, Frederic. *Arranging and Describing Archives and Manuscripts.* Chicago: Society of American Archivists, 1990.

Minchew, Kaye Lanning. *Archives for Local Governments.* Local Government Records Management Technical Publication Series, edited by Julian L. Mims III. Rancho Cucamonga, CA: MCEF, IIMC and NAGARA, 2012.

Minnesota Historical Society, *Electronic Records Management Guidelines—Digital Storage.* Accessed October 27, 2015. http://www.mnhs.org/preserve/records/electronicrecords/erstorage.php#guidelines

National Archives and Records Administration (NARA). *Records Schedule Review Process.* Accessed August 25, 2015. http://www.archives.gov/records-mgmt/policy/records-schedule-review-process.html

National Archives and Records Administration (NARA). *Memorandum NARA 1571, Archival Storage Standards.* Washington, DC: The National Archives, 2001.

Nelson, Terry B. "Managing Electronic Records." Local Government Records Management Technical Publication Series, edited by Julian L. Mims III. Rancho Cucamonga, CA: MCEF, IIMC and NAGARA, 2012.

Multnomah County Code. Records Management, Archival and Storage, § 8.500–8.502, Chapter 8, "County Assets." Revised October 2, 2014.

Northeast Document Conservation Center. "Low Cost/No Cost Improvements in Climate Control." Accessed October 13, 2015. https://www.nedcc.org/free-resources/preservation-leaflets/2.-the-environment/2.6-low-cost-no-cost-improvements-in-climate-control.

O'Toole, James M., and Richard J. Cox. *Understanding Archives and Manuscripts.* Archival Fundamentals Series II. Chicago: Society of American Archivists, 2006.

Pacifico, Michele F., and Thomas P. Wilsted. *Archival and Special Collections Facilities: Guidelines for Archivists, Librarians, Architects, and Engineers.* Chicago: Society of American Archivists, 2009.

Pearce-Moses, Richard. *A Glossary of Archival and Records Terminology.* Chicago: Society of American Archivists, 2005. Accessed August 2015. http://www2.archivists.org/glossary.

Pugh, Mary Jo. *Providing Reference Service for Archives and Manuscripts.* Archival Fundamental Series. Chicago: Society of American Archivists, 2005.

Ritzenthaler, Mary Lynn, and Diane Vogt O'Connor. *Photographs: Archival Care and Management.* Chicago: Society of American Archivists, 2006.

Ritzenhaler, Mary Lynn. *Preserving Archives and Manuscripts*. 2nd edition. Chicago: Society of American Archivists, 2010.

Roe, Kathleen. *Arranging and Describing Archives and Manuscripts*. Archival Fundamentals Series II. Chicago: Society of American Archivists, 2005.

Rutherford County (TN) Archives. Accessed July 2014. http://www.rutherfordcoun tytn.gov/archives/index.htm.

Schellenberg, T. R. *Modern Archives: Principles and Techniques.* Chicago: University of Chicago Press, 1956.

Slate, John H. *Identifying and Locating Your Records*. Local Government Records Management Technical Publication Series, edited by Julian L. Mims III. Rancho Cucamonga, CA: MCEF, IIMC and NAGARA, 2012.

Theimer, Kate, ed. *Outreach: Innovative Practices for Archives and Special Collections*. Lanham, MD: Rowman & Littlefield, 2014.

Tuin, Stephanie. *Managing Records on Limited Resources*. Local Government Records Management Technical Publication Series, edited by Julian L. Mims III. Rancho Cucamonga, CA: MCEF, IIMC and NAGARA, 2012.

U.S. Census Bureau. *2002 Census of Governments, Vol 1, Number 1, Government Organization*. Washington, DC: U.S. Government Printing Office, 2002.

Wilsted, Thomas P., *Planning New and Remodeled Archival Facilities.* Chicago: Society of American Archivists, 2007.

Wilsted, Tom. *The Selection and Development of Local Government Records Storage Facilities*. Local Government Records Management Technical Publication Series, edited by Julian L. Mims III. Rancho Cucamonga, CA: MCEF, IIMC and NAGARA, 2011.

Wojcik, Caryn, Greg Colton, and Brice Sample. *Using and Storing Microfilm*. Local Government Records Management Technical Publication Series, edited by Julian L. Mims III. Rancho Cucamonga, CA: MCEF, IIMC and NAGARA, 2012.

Wosh, Peter J., and Russell D. James. *Public Relations and Marketing for Archives: A How-to-Do-It Manual*. Chicago: Society of American Archivists and Neal-Schuman Publishers, 2011.

Zamon, Christina J. *The Lone Arranger: Succeeding in a Small Repository*. Chicago: Society of American Archivists, 2012.

# Index

Page references for figures and photographs are italicized.

# About the Authors

**John H. Slate** is city archivist for the city of Dallas, where he has been responsible for historic city government records in the Dallas Municipal Archives since 2000. He is a member of the Academy of Certified Archivists and possesses a BS from the University of Texas at Austin and a master's degree in library and information science, specializing in archival enterprise, from the same institution.

John's work in archives, libraries, and special collections began at the Briscoe Center for American History at the University of Texas at Austin, where he spent thirteen years. He previously was curator/librarian at the Hertzberg Museum of the San Antonio Public Library and also was archivist at the Texas African American Photography Archive in Dallas. He is past chair of the Government Records and the Visual Materials Sections of the Society of American Archivists, as well as chair of its Local Government Records Round Table. He served as president of the Society of Southwest Archivists, 2010–2011. In addition he is a multi-term member of the Texas State Library and Archives Commission's Historical Records Advisory Board.

Slate has written numerous articles on archives, photography, music, and Texas history and is the author or coauthor of four Arcadia Images of America series books: *Historic Dallas Parks*, *Lost Austin*, *Dealey Plaza*, and *John F. Kennedy Sites in Dallas-Fort Worth*.

**Kaye Lanning Minchew** works as a consultant in archives and historic preservation. She served as executive director of the Troup County Historical Society in LaGrange, Georgia, from 1985 until 2015, where she oversaw operations of the Troup County Archives and Legacy Museum on Main. She received a bachelor of arts in history from the University of North Carolina at Asheville, and master of arts in history and master of library science from the University of North Carolina at Chapel Hill. She was named a fellow of the Society of American Archivists in 2011 and of the Society of Georgia Archivists in 2009. She testified before Congress about the National Historical Publications and Records Commission in 2010 on behalf of the National Association of Government Archives and Records Administrators.

Minchew has been a member of the Georgia Historical Records Advisory Board since 1993 and is the president of the Friends of Georgia Archives. She served as cochair of the Coalition to Preserve the Georgia Archives and helped lead the fight to keep the Georgia Archives open to the public in 2012–2013. She serves on the National Historical Publications and Records Commission. She is recipient of the Georgia Historical Records Advisory Board Lifetime Achievement Award, 2007. Her book *A President in Our Midst: Franklin Delano Roosevelt in Georgia* was published by the University of Georgia Press in 2016.